# A JOURNEY BEYOND EXPECTATIONS

## BY

## AZHAR MAJID QURESHI

Published in 2018 by:
BCH Sdn Bhd
Unit 1-17-1 , Menara Bangkok Bank
Berjaya Central Park
No.105 Jalan Ampang
50450 Kuala Lumpur . Malaysia
E-Mail : aznie@pd.jaring.asia



First Edition  2018

Perpustakaan Negara Malaysia
Library of Congress Cataloging-in-Publication Data
A Journey Beyond Expectations/ Azhar Majid Qureshi
Includes indexes

ISBN 978-967-16633-0-1

# CONTENT

**_ACKNOLWDGEMENTS_**

_I dedicate this book to my parents Dr. Abdul Majid Qureshi and Dr. Amina Qureshi who supported me to fulfill all my dreams. Also, to the love of my life my wife Annie who has stood by me in the toughest trials of this life._

# INTRODUCTION

Most of the published non – fiction books are written by and for the famous people. Some of these books are an inspiration for masses and perhaps others reveal the darker side of life.  A few words cannot encapsulate the essence of such books and the deep impact that these have on many people and many facets of life.

What are the prospects for a book written by an ordinary person about his journey through life, the trials and triumphs such as experienced by perhaps 95 % of the world's population ? Would someone actually publish such a book? Even if such a book is ever published would people actually read it? If people did read it, perhaps many would relate to the different narrations and statements. Others would vehemently disagree with the content and dismiss it as utter rubbish. Yet, it might arouse sufficient interest to make the author's effort a worthwhile undertaking.

Perhaps the whole idea is based on an absurd notion that publishers and people in general have the time to consider the views of an ordinary person. However, I believe that this book will be published sooner or later for the diversity of its content. The fact that the content and layout is so absurd that this very fact will become the quintessence of the book. After all the content is aimed at the majority of the population of this earth and a reminder to everyone that dreams can come true. Life is a very complex matter and we all face prejudices and bigotry but if you maintain the straight path you can overcome all hurdles and make this journey a pleasant one.

The book is written overwhelmingly with a British perspective but due to an International flavor it will appeal to people all over the world .e.g. the chapter that narrates the recent British history in simple words and a very concise form; or the incidents when the author faced natural calamities as earthquakes, volcanic eruptions and unbelievable tragedies, may in time become popular reading material.

The main objective of the book is to share with as many people as possible some sensitive subjects derived from the experience of a fairly average person. It may help readers to understand the topics as these are narrated in very simple terms.

This book narrates the journey of the author through many countries experiencing many cultures. This book is not a Lonely Planet guide, as some chapters may imply. However, this book covers more than just the exotic locations and sights. In simple words it gives an insight into the history of some of the exotic countries like Mexico and Peru. There is an insight provided into the history of China in simple terms so that the ordinary people can read and absorb the content. It narrates the experience of doing business in China and South East Asian, the protocols, business etiquette, business relationships, religious and cultural sensitivities.

Most chapters of this book have a tinge of humour in spite of the very serious topics that are discussed. The chapter on RACE, RELIGION AND CONFLICT is a simple explanation on some very sensitive issues. It is felt that people need to get simple explanations for the issues that are raging around the world and creating misunderstanding and social conflict.

One of the most meaningful chapters will be the author's attempt to explain his relationship with the United Kingdom. It may be one of the very few occasions that an Asian not born in Britain puts a positive spin on his time and working life in a country that he is proud to be associated with. Furthermore, the author has derived a simple version of the recent British history and how it has shaped life over the years.

The passage of life, in his own words will reflect on the many changes faced by the human race in the relevant period and will take a gentle 'stroll ' looking at the many technological advances in this lifetime. Everyone is aware of such advances but there is no harm to remind to ourselves.

While so many diverse topics are covered the central theme remains firm that this book is written by a humble and an ordinary man and hopefully everyone will find something of interest in this compilation.

# BORN TO TRAVEL

*...nothing so liberalizes a man and expands the kindly instincts that nature put in him as travel and contact with many kinds of people. (Mark Twain)*

It is a known fact that mankind from its renaissance has always had the urge to travel and likes to see what lies beyond the immediate horizon. There have always been and always will be a variety of reasons which will encourage and enforce travel. There are no longer limits to the perceived destinations and who knows before too long the commercial travel to the surrounding planets will become a routine matter.

As Mark Twain has profoundly put it that travel may well be the answer to removing prejudices, bigotry and other cultural misunderstandings. Who knows?

However, in the past travel has had a dark side too in terms of Colonization, Slavery, spreading of deadly diseases, exploitation of natural and mineral resources etc.

The above words are very bland and nothing new about the statements but these are put in to lay a base for what is to come.

Without delving too deep in the negative side let me highlight the positive aspects of travel and that too in a lighter vein.

From the time I can remember life which would be about from five years of age I really wanted to travel. In those days there was no TV available where I lived let alone Internet or even the notion of it. The only mediums to put people in touch with the outside world were the Radio, Books and Magazines. I did listen to the radio but most of what I heard was beyond my understanding. I could just about read at that age but could see pictures and certainly my father used to read to me about distant countries and strange cultures from the National Geographic or the Readers Digest magazines. I was always fascinated to hear fairy tales in different settings which did not make sense at the time. The tales of Aladin and Ali Baba and the rest of the fascinating accounts of the magical imagination as narrated by relatives were a source of great inspiration.

My family travelled a great deal within the country and my father being a senior employee of the Railways entitled us to travel in style. As a legacy of the Colonial days and inherited from the then departed British, the Senior officials were allocated their own rail carriages complete with bedrooms , lounge , dining room , balcony , kitchen and servant quarters. These carriages were hitched on to the trains for the privileged few as and when they wanted to travel. In spite of such privileges something in me was not satisfied and I wanted something more and I was not even sure what it was.

The other impact on my life was that the schools I attended were run by Missionaries and this did lead to some knowledge of other faiths and other countries.

By the age of seven I could read well and enjoyed looking at the National Geographic and Readers Digest magazines and started to understand the Continents and the Solar system not that I ever wanted to go into orbit .

Perhaps when I was six years old my father took me to see a Hollywood movie. The film's title was Vera Cruz set in Mexico. In spite of the somewhat violent content, I was simply fascinated with some of the colourful aspects of Mexico. That at the age of six! This fascination was something very private and I did not dare discuss with anyone. There and then I wanted to visit Mexico and that desire almost became an obsession for years to come. Only I did not know how that could be possible at that time, travelling Overseas was only a distant fantasy for most people.  Unbeknown to me at the time, fate was already plotting to get me to Mexico and the first step was taken when my father decided to further his career as a Medical Doctor and go to the UK for enhanced Diploma in Tropical Medicine and Hygiene.

I have traced as to why my father was so keen to give up his very stable and prestigious life in his country and uproot the family to move abroad. He in turn also had an urge from his young years to explore the world. For him the flash point was when his uncle went to Great Britain in the 1930s and came back with wonderful stories of the voyage. Of course in those days the journey was a tough, three weeks at sea in perhaps not the top class of travel. The travel by sea necessitated calls at many fascinating ports. I have to add that my paternal grandfather and his brother (the one who went to UK) were eminent 'Hakims' of their time in the city of Sialkot in the sub-continent. The Wikipedia definition of a Hakim: In Pakistan and India, Hakim or Hakeem denotes a herbal medicine practitioner, specially of 'Unani' medicine. Unani medicine is the term for Perso-Arabic traditional medicine as practiced in Mughal India and in Muslim cultures in South Asia and modern day Central Asia. The term Unānī means "Greek"as the Perso-Arabic system of medicine was based on the teachings of the Greek physicians Hippocrates and Galen. To attain a status of Hakim one had to go through years of learning and training with the most famous Hakims before they were allowed to set up on their own. My father's uncle actually travelled to Great Britain after being invited as a part of a select group to present the sub-continent's traditional Medicines details and historical insights in the evolution of this art/science. Of course my parents were both trained as Western Medical Doctors and they practiced their skills successfully and with distinction in many countries.

One thing led to another and soon with a sense of great excitement I was leaving the shores of the country where I was born and unto the unknown. I was still a long way from Mexico but the vital first few steps had been taken. Many 'Mr.Bean' like moments occurred in the initial stages of the travel abroad but some of these will be re-counted later. It was a privilege to travel to many countries across many continents and this definitely broadened the mind and hidden linguistic abilities came to the fore and this was indeed a surprise.

Eventually, at the age of thirty the thrilling moment arrived as  landed in Mexico City and went on to spend a number of years in that exotic country. That moment in time I felt very privileged and perhaps this ordinary man became special for just that moment.  I visited the city of Vera Cruz  while working in the Oil & Gas industry and in fact I ended up spending most of my time in the other Oil city of Mexico i.e. Villahermosa.

Looking back, I am grateful that a dream that I had as a child turned into reality and the ambition that I had to travel has been fulfilled. I have travelled to over eighty four countries of the world and visited almost all the places that I wanted to. I still have the will to travel and especially to the countries I have never been to.

Naturally, I did not spend a great deal of time in some of these countries but took the time to learn what I could. In the countries where I did live for longer periods I did make it a point to absorb myself in the local way of life. In other words I always ate the local food with some exceptions, I drank the local specialties, I socialized like a local person, I loved and romanced like a local person and most important of all I adhered to the local laws and regulations.

It is a remarkable fact and in my case true, that if an individual really wants something with true passion then the fate and the universe will unite to make it happen. I believe most human beings do get this kind of a break at least once in their lifetime but need a lot of luck to exploit the opportunity when it comes.

*EARLY DAYS IN NIGERIA WITH THE FAMILY*

*GRANDFATHER - HAKIM ABDUL AZIZ*

# RACE, RELIGON – CONFLICT

(…..Racism is man's gravest threat to man – the maximum of hatred for a minimum of reason – Alexander)

## RACE

To belong to a particular race is the greatest gift bestowed on human beings by the Creator. Each race has a right to be proud of their own identity. Unfortunately, the history of the world clearly indicates that some races have believed themselves to be superior to the other races. It is not only the white race who are guilty of such prejudice. When each race starts to hold and skew this superiority, racism also starts to affect and influence the balance and dynamics of the human race.

I certainly believe that Racism is evil and has created much conflict and suffering for mankind. It is still very much live and in spite of all the universal efforts to eliminate racial bigotry the negative feelings and hatred remains in the hearts of each and every one of us. Let us be honest we are uncomfortable with other beings of different colour or creed. Some of us are more tolerant than others but if truth be known, deep down each of us is a racist.

I was born with a brown skin but to the world at large I am just another Black person. It took me a long time to realize that I was considered a black person by most white people and that in itself proves that sub – consciously I was considering myself superior to certain races and hence a racist. It takes guts to admit this underlying tendency so prevalent in every human being.

For White people to have some degree of discomfort with all the other races of the world is one issue. However, it is very hard to understand the bigotry of the darker and the yellow people.

To illustrate this point, let me highlight the hatred to varying degrees of the sub-continent Asians towards the black race. Can this be denied? The answer is an overwhelming NO. Can we say that the African – American people actually consider the people of the Caribbean and the black people of Africa as equals to them? The answer is an overwhelming NO. Do the different black races in Africa consider other people with same coloured skin as equals? NO.

Do the Arabs consider any race as their equals? NO. Do the Japanese consider any other race in Asia or for that matter on this earth as their equals? NO. Is there total harmony and equality amongst the different regional Chinese? NO. Is there racial harmony in the rest of South East Asia. NO. ? Is there racial harmony in the sub-continent? NO. Instead there is the Caste system, tribal and feudal loyalties, regional conflict leading to 'racial hatred'. Are the multi-racial populations in Latin America living in total harmony? NO.

In the year 2017, USA's attitude to race and the Islamic religion is a very hot topic. The US President of the time is being lambasted by the whole world and one has to say that his blunt attitude does not really do his image any favours. Whatever be the case, does it make all the white Americans racists including the President? No

Most American citizens who have had some experience of overseas travel are wonderful people. I have always mixed well with Americans and found their approach to life very open, they are eager to learn and understand the other races of this world. They have very special qualities in terms of generosity, humour and social graces. Of course their history shows a terrible record in terms of racial hatred and excesses committed in the past, these were simply deplorable. Various US governments for many reasons have ended up interfering in the affairs of other sovereign states and sometimes the whole regions. This has invariably created hatred for the USA but there is no reason to hate every US citizen. Even today a great number of people in the USA are insular in that they never travel outside their own state let alone the country and hence are most likely to be influenced by the media and other negative reports. By all means everyone has a right and if it means through personal experience they dislike Americans then so be it. However, does it mean that the whole nation must be hated sufficiently to target them for mindless violence? I say no and I wish the violent and barbaric acts against innocent people are stopped, then we may get a better understanding in this world. The Americans for their part believe that for too long they have carried the burdens of the world and played their part to defend the rights and freedom of the human race and always paid a price for it. Arguments and debates will go on for years on the viewpoints of both sides but a point has been put forward for the whole world to consider.

Some special cases in point are mentioned:

SOUTH AFRICA - A remarkable turnaround in their apartheid practises and an incredible piece of History has been created. No attempt is made to comment on the changes experienced by the Rainbow nation except to say that we live in hope.

AUSTRALIA - A country that was at one extreme of White dominance and forever living in fear of being invaded by the Chinese. They almost annihilated the indigenous population but had to review their policies once the Vietnamese boat people were thrust upon them? Gone are the 'Whites only' immigration policies. This country has very liberal policies and the regulatory framework is continuously being improved to ensure equal rights of all its citizens. Within the society the tolerance levels have undergone much change. However, there are still the extreme racists and bigots within the society. At this time the Australian Government seems to be taking retro- grade steps and once again profiling Immigration. This is due to the current Islamophobia and the abundance of refugees seeking new places to settle.

MALAYSIA – The only truly multi-racial society in the world. The diversity gives this country an incredible status as one of the most colourful and exotic places on this earth. However, there are certain tensions within the Malay, Chinese and Indian races which can be understood. The Government of Malaysia does a great job in maintaining this harmony.

Having been so bombastic about a very complex issue, I have to clarify and narrate personal experiences.

By and large I have got away without being a victim of the mindless racism. In fact I have been victimized by my own kind who always classed me too dark to be the son of a mother whose lineage was from the people of Kashmir. The people of Kashmir are the Aryans of the sub-continent population. I came

Across one or two racial chants directed at me and that was about it. I lived for fourteen years in the city of Lincoln, UK. I felt very comfortable in that city and the surrounding area. In fact my best friends are three generations of a family living in the Metheringham Fen. I can meet them whenever, I do get a chance and the warmth is the same as ever. One could say that friendship is a human bond that transcends all colour and religion. I do not want to sound unrealistic as my own experience is a rare privilege through the locations I lived in and the life style I pursued.

Furthermore, in my working life I was judged on my merit and any progress or the lack of it was based on personal attitude and performance. It was once in my life when I needed a change of career that I realized that I had to work more than twice as hard as the mainstream people in the UK to get a position befitting my qualifications and experience.

United Kingdom has strengthened the regulatory framework to promote equality and eliminate racism. Considerable progress has been made. My daughter born in 1989 in the city of Lincoln has a different view on racism and bigotry. She has spent most of her life in Birmingham and is totally a patriotic Brit.

On the other hand, there still exist definite problems in the society and people are left behind on account of their race and there is suffering for a great many people termed as the ethnic minorities. Things are getting better and there is hope. However, racism will never be entirely eliminated.

## RELIGON

Religion is a matter of personal choice and having a belief is not such a bad thing. Religion is meant to be the guidance for human beings and society. Alas religion has turned out to be the basis of historical and prolonged conflict and suffering.

Everyone must have the right to choose their path and if it were so, there would be less conflict.

I am at peace with my religion. How I used to wish there was better awareness of Islam in the Western world when I first migrated. Tragically, the awareness when it came was very negative beyond my or anyone's imagination. How could a religion that believes in Adam and Eve, Abraham, Noah, Moses, Solmon and David, Jesus and all the other Biblical prophets be so misunderstood. A religion based on human equality, tolerance and forgiveness has been totally misrepresented. This is due to the small number of fanatics who have defied every principle of humanity and with mindless violence changed the perception of this religion to as low as it could go.

The Muslim scholars need to work on an interpretation of the Quran which truly reflects the values and principles of Islam. At the moment the only message that is being conveyed is of violence and hatred. There are more than 1.4 bn Muslims in the world and a great many of these are highly sophisticated and educated people. Surely, they have the sense to practise a logical religion .If they were all fanatics and fundamentalist's life would not be worth living. A minority of perhaps a few thousand are distorting the image of this religion. It will take many years of hard work by modern scholars and the relevant authorities to eliminate the problems that exist. This is not a simplistic view but a hope and a prayer that perhaps will not be realized in my lifetime. The vast population of Muslims could do with being educated and given a sense of belonging in the new world order.

Some of the regional and political conflicts occurring in the Middle East, Africa and Afghanistan are not entirely caused by the difference of opinion with the West. There are many complex internal conflicts based on tribal allegiances and the different factions of Islam. Some of these conflicts have not been clearly understood by the West when they set about judging the violence. It would not be possible to analyse each conflict but some of the main factors are highlighted.

In Africa, tribal allegiances even transcend the religious affiliations. That applies to some extent within Afghanistan but of course the vast majority of people share the same religion but they will fight each other over tribal conflicts.

There are two main factions within the Muslim religion . Sunni and Shia based on allegiance to succession of leadership through consensus or the Prophet's lineage. These two factions have clashed for centuries and most of the time violently. The majority of Muslims in the world belong to the Sunni Faction. In the modern Day geographical sense: Saudi Arabia is dominantly Sunni and they see themselves as the protectors of Islam. Most of Africa, Pakistan, Malaysia, and Indonesia etc also belong to the Majority faction. The simplest and practical interpretation of Islam in my opinion is practised in Malaysia and Indonesia. However, certain changes taking place in some other countries will lead to a more tolerant nations and hopefully in time a better perception of the Muslims.

Iran and Iraq both are Majority Shia countries. Shia's also have a sizeable population in Pakistan and also have large communities in Turkey and the Middle East. To make it more complex, the Late Iraqi leader Saddam Hussein was a Sunni leading a majority Shia nation. In some way that is why he had to rule with a very heavy hand as there was always conflict amongst his people. Iran and Iraq fought a significant War for eight years in the 80's. Both countries belonged to the same religious faction but political hostilities prevailed. Some of the current conflicts are along this factional conflict. Soon after Iraq was 'liberated'   the coalition forces had to face a lot of armed action from the different religious groups plus nationalists plus regional backed militia and Al-Qaeda. Many of these were the Shite groups emerging after the demise of Saddam and wanted to ensure that they were not going to be suppressed by the Minority Sunni population ever again. The so called Islamic State terrorists took a significant part in this conflict being Sunnis they opposed the pre-dominantly Western coalition and the Shias. They gained notoriety for their ruthless and cruel regime and took large swathes of Iraqi and Syrian territory. They introduced barbaric rules and regulations that were their own concepts and philosophy and nothing to do with the teachings of Islam.

Another example is Syria, a majority Sunni country but ruled by the Assad family who belong to a distinct Shia clan. What started as a pro –democracy movement has become a very complex conflict. The conflict involves the ISIS, Al Qaeda, Iranian backed militias, Saudi backed militias and for good measure the Western alliance's backing the rebels and Russia backing the Assad regime. All this is very complex and a deeper study of the conflict is needed before proper judgement and total blame put on Islam for these type of violent conflicts. . I just wish Muslims Sunni or Shia would stop killing and harming each other. Much of this is up to the Religious scholars to teach their factions the true meaning of Islam.

# THE ASTOUNDING EVENTS OF THE LAST 65 YEARS

......History can carry on no successful competition with news, in the matter of sharp interest. When an eye-witness sets down in narrative form some extraordinary occurrence which he has witnessed, that is news -- that is the news form, and its interest is absolutely indestructible; time can have no deteriorating effect upon that episode.

- Autobiographical dictation, 15 January 1906. Published in Autobiography of Mark Twain, Vol. 1 (University of California Press, 2010)

Historical events always have an impact on the lives of each and every human being, whether this happens directly or indirectly but for sure there are always ripple effects for everyone. Most interesting thing about history is that certain events keep repeating themselves. Other events which do not have significant importance at the time of occurrence turn out to be profound and long term. As an example of the two statements (a) Regional wars and conflicts keep on recurring (b) who would have thought that the commodity Crude Oil would become one single parameter whose price rise and fall would determine the economic state of the world.

A few years before I was born some significant events took place. One was the ending of the World War II which ended one of the most violent chapters in the human history. However , it created two large blocks of differing ideology and no sooner peace had been made the seeds were laid for future large scale conflict. The second was the creation of the state of Israel. From my point this needed to happen and the Jewish people definitely needed a sovereign state of their own. However, the super powers should have thought through the consequences of doing this in a bit of a rush. There should have been more dialogue with the people of Palestine whose land was carved up and the Muslim world at large who were all incensed with this outcome. Another event which affected the lives of some 500 m people at that time was the hastened partition of India based on religious lines. Two countries emerged India and Pakistan. To complicate matters Pakistan had two parts the West and the East separated by 1500 miles of the

Indian Territory and the respective people were only bound by religion but with distinct cultures and different languages and social norms.

When I was born, the Korean War was raging and it was a direct consequence of the first of the events mentioned above. At the end of the war Communist Russia soon established itself as the mighty Union of Soviet Socialist Republic and set about imposing its ideology on the rest of the world. A number of Eastern European states were set up as satellites of this regime and any unrest or opposition in any one of these was cruelly crushed. The most notorious symbol of this discord was the Berlin Wall where a city well within the Republic of East Germany firmly under the control of USSR had a part of it under the control of the USA and the West! How could such a thing ever happen? If anything this kept the conflict live on a 24 hour 365 days a year and Berlin was somewhat of a centre stage

USSR tried to spread its influence around the globe and even attempted to set up a nuclear missile facility in Cuba right on the door step of the USA. It was one of the many times that the world was on the edge as the two powers faced off in a very sensitive geographical spot.

The so called Cold War was played by both sides and no one wanted to step back. The USSR spread its influence in Asia and as they did share the ideology with China even in spite of many differences a great amount of support in terms of technology and armaments and food flowed from the former to the latter. The prolonged conflict that had been plaguing Vietnam for many decades become a conflict of Communism vs the US bloc with huge suffering for the human beings. Cambodia got embroiled in this overall ideological war and in its attempt to become an agrarian society butchered half its own population. Malaysia had to fight an internal war for over thirty years to ensure that the communists were eliminated from its shores. In Indonesia a very bloody civil unrest took place to stop the communists. The Soviet Union influenced many Arab nations using the pro – Israel policies of the US and the West as an contention to win favours. The Soviet influence also spread its influence to many other countries in Africa. Latin America was one continent which became a region where the ideology of the

Soviets mixed with the local politics became an acclaimed cause leading to many armed conflicts, overthrow of legitimate regimes, military dictatorships and general instability suppressing the much needed economic growth and prosperity.

The world was in real danger of being dominated by the Communist influence and many of the current generation do not realize how the left wing penetrated the established democracy within the United Kingdom. There were serious concerns for some years and many conspiracy theories abounded about right wing planned coups to take over the Parliament. French politics were dominated by the left wing policies. The US fought this cold war tooth and nail as restlessness grew due to the direct involvement in the war in Vietnam, the rise of the Civil Liberty action at home and the alleged penetration of strategic institutions by the communists. One of the US institution that led this fight was the Central Intelligence Agency and the process to defend American interests it committed many grave accesses that led to further unnecessary conflicts.

In the meantime, while the Cold War was at its peak, the US faced growing unrest at home by the protests related to the Civil Liberties and Equal rights for the African American movements. One of the great personalities of the last century Dr.Martin Luther King gained eminence for his passion and the peaceful marches to raise awareness of this issue. Sadly, he met a violent end and was assassinated before he could complete his mission. Nevertheless, his legacy in due course brought about many changes in the US society.

On the other front the USSR faced very strong sanctions and decided to invade Afghanistan in the last 70s at a very unstable time for the world. The invasion proved to be very costly for the Soviets and the mighty Union started to crumble.

It did not take very long after that for the Soviet Union to disintegrate and whilst the Communists retained influence the Cold War was over and there was only one clear winner and that was the USA. The free world had overcome an evil force but did that bring Peace, the answer is sadly NO.

The Cold War cost billions of Dollars, invention of Evil and loathsome weapons. Lot of unnecessary deaths and suffering imposed on innocent people. The world has not learnt from this episode.

The creation of Israel led to many regional and global conflicts and perhaps the seeds of modern Islamist Terrorism were sown as a result. Israel has every right to exist and defend itself against forces trying to destroy it. They have defended themselves very well every time they have been threatened. The surrounding Arab countries have never agreed a common policy amongst themselves with reference to Israel and hence it has left an unfinished conflict creating violent organizations who have become more evil with time. Who is funding the terrorists? Who is training them to become stronger? Fingers point in every direction but no one dares to accuse the rich and the powerful. There have been many efforts towards peace but there is no end in sight.

In 1947, the British granted independence to the sub-continent creating two nations, Pakistan and India along the religious and communal lines. The ownership of one of the most strategic state i.e. Kashmir was left undecided. Kashmir houses part of the Himalayas that provide the sources of all rivers into the sub-continent and is a land of great natural beauty. On top of that the population of Kashmir is dominantly Muslim. Immediately both sides claimed the state and the there was an armed conflict straightaway even when there was ongoing chaos with the finalization of the border lines, moving millions of Hindus, Muslim and Sikhs from their homes to new locations. Hundreds and thousands of people were massacred by each side in the frustration and anger that followed. There are heart wrenching tales of families being split up and in other cases being butchered. My own ancestors were directly involved in this forced migration and ended up all over the new country and only miracles re-united them all. In 1947 there were no real telephone lines and the postal system did not function, addresses were ill defined. My mother was separated from her family and ended up in a strong Sikh enclave which was a bad scenario for a young Muslim woman. However, her life and honour was spared and in fact she was escorted safely to a group of Muslim refugees on the way to the border to cross into Pakistan. The reason being that she was a Doctor of Medicine and had served the Sikh community well and in the end they showed their gratitude. After crossing the border she had no idea which way to head because she had no contact with any of the other members of the family who had crossed earlier. Only by a miracle she bumped into her father who was just wandering and searching for her at all the crossing points and that day happened to be at the one where she arrived. There are countless painful stories of this type and similar scenarios have been re-enacted in different parts of the world with fleeing refugees in violent conflicts.

In my opinion a full scale partition should have been avoided as it carved up a great country and created conflict among the people who had the same culture, the same physical appearance but different religions. There was of course a strong possibility that the Majority Hindu population backed by the Sikhs would have suppressed the minority of Muslims in an undivided India but some form of confederation may have been the answer. The Hindus were undoubtedly better placed to manage the nation as they had accepted the Western Education and occupied senior Government positions and were better business men and overall were much more prosperous then the Muslims. Muslims had not helped themselves by rejecting the Western Education, especially for their women. (My grandfather must have been an exceptional man to send two of his four daughters to study Western medicine in mixed sex colleges). However the two new countries were in conflict from the start and have actually never really stopped. It is worth noting that at the time of partition a significant number of Muslims, perhaps 40% of the overall decided to stay on in India. Over the years perhaps they have not always been treated fairly but have survived and now are beginning to move forward.

India being the larger country retained the democratic principles and after many decades of economic struggles it has arrived on the Global platform as a significant nation. Education and retaining English as the medium has played a major part in its apparent success. Amongst other achievements, its skilled people are now located in every part of the world offering their expertise. The technological development within India has been astonishing and a credit to the country and its people. In the end Democracy no matter how distorted it maybe, wins. With a population of 1.3bn people, India has a say in global matters.

Economic prosperity is evident with a rising middle class. With an ancient colourful culture and many traditions it is an amazing hotpot of sub-cultures and is a major tourist country. The conflict with Pakistan over Kashmir has led to many wars with Pakistan. India has managed to handle itself adequately each time and in the early 70s succeeded in dis–membering Pakistan by invading it Eastern part and creating the third nation of the sub-continent, Bangladesh.

Pakistan for its part was set up as a Muslim nation but was meant to be a secular society, it has not worked out the way it was planned. Through a serious of Military dictatorships and corrupt civil Governments, Pakistan has not made the progress it was capable of making. Religious fundamentalism on the rise since the 70s has hampered progress. The conflict with India is a bigger burden for Pakistan which maintains an abnormally large size of Armed forces and has to bear an absurd defence budget. Of course the Armed forces are an integral part of the leadership in Pakistan and are not likely to diminish themselves. In order to maintain their hold on the nation it is said that some factions within ensure that the tension with India will never diminish. Both India and Pakistan have nuclear capabilities and this remains a very serious concern for all concerned.

The greatest shame is that after many serious Peace efforts the situation is as it was seventy years ago. Both countries expend billions of Dollars to maintain readiness for a potential armed conflict. India in spite of its great progress has pockets of abject poverty and it could do with eliminating these. The infra structure in India does not match the swagger and style of the country and needs much more development. Whilst part of the society has moved on the stigma of the caste system still shrouds the thinking of millions. The rural areas remain mired in century old beliefs and prejudices. In fact both the countries suffer from feudal domination in the rural areas which lead to abuse of the human rights of the people struggling on less than earnings of US$ 50 per month for their hard physical toil.

India has a population of 1.32 bn and will soon overtake China as the most populous nation. Pakistan has population of 200 m and Bangladesh has a population of 162 m. Combined population of about 1.7 bn which is more than

20% of the cumulative total of the world's population. As an idealist, how I wish that there was a way that they could all make peace and live in harmony and that could lead to this part of the world becoming an Economic powerhouse. They should look at the example of the people of Vietnam who had serious and violent conflict externally and internally for over a hundred years but now live in peace with each other and the result is the country is making significant Economic progress.

Meanwhile, other events in other countries shaped the period under review. For many years Iran a strategically located country was ruled by Reza Shah Phalvi a ruler friendly to the US and the West. Iran was a buffer for the West against the Soviet Union entering the Persian Gulf which was the sensitive area supplying Oil & Gas to the US and the West. In the 70s Iran was a very prosperous country as it was one of the leading producer of Oil & Gas. The ruler was driving Iran towards total modernization and Westernization. He was a ruthless autocrat and over the years the opposition consisting of a disillusioned and a bitter population plus the orthodox Shia clergy started to get the masses to listen to them. The Iranian revolution started with small scale demonstrations in the early 70s growing into a total uprising, forcing the Shah to flee the country and paving the way for the Shiite Spiritual Leader Ayatullah Kohemini to return from exile and take over the reins of this country. Strict Shria laws were imposed and in a bloody bath all those that condoned the Shah, his regime and all his allies were brutally executed. The whole world was rocked from the aftershocks of this revolution. The US and the West lost a major ally and a solid supplier of a significant part of their energy requirements. The whole of the Middle East was destabilized and that was about the time that the Soviet Union walked in and invaded Afghanistan with firm eyes on Iran and the Persian Gulf.

The relationship between Iran and the West deteriorated leading to an controversial occupation and holding of US Embassy staff  as hostages by Iran'student's for almost a year and a half.

As for the Iranians:

 Views differ on the impact of the revolution. For some it was "the most significant, hopeful and profound event in the entirety of contemporary Islamic history,"while other Iranians believe that the revolution was a time when"for a few years we all lost our minds", and which "promised us heaven, but... created a hell on earth."

In order to aggravate the enmity with Iran, the West aided and encouraged the Iraqi dictator, Saddam Hussein to attack Iran. Another unnecessary war raged for seven odd years. It sort of took the intensity out of the Iranian revolution. Without this conflict to occupy their minds maybe there would have been further regional upheaval. The unhappy consequence of this regional interference was that Saddam Hussein and his regime became stronger and he started to create mischief around the region. All this came to a head as Iraq invaded the oil rich state of Kuwait and threatened Saudi Arabia right at its borders. The world protested but Saddam remained defiant.

In the meantime Soviet Union had gone through one of the most discreditable periods of its history when it withdrew all its forces from Afghanistan. The US and West hailed this as a major victory probably the most decisive of the Cold War. The immediate consequences of this were: The Mujahadeen or the freedom fighters who had been heavily sponsored by the USA with arms and cash had no more armed conflict on their hand and after a decade of Soviet rule they set about trying to gain control of the war ravaged country. This was the emergence of Al –Qaeda and Osama bin Laden who had both been recipients of generous aid to fight the Soviets suddenly started to look at USA as the enemy. Pakistan which was the conduit country to take drugs from Afghanistan and purchase arms from the West and also housed the main CIA activities also became an unstable country. The ready availability of arms and drugs was a bad recipe. The fundamentalists also seized the opportunity to raise their profile in a situation where there was a lot of political confusion. The Government of Pakistan was clearly benefitting from the US generosity towards the Afghans as this had to be routed through this regime. The fundamentalists presented themselves as an alternative to the influence of US which was by then being termed as the enemy of Islam thanks to the prolonged hate campaigns by the Palestinians and the Iranians.

At the same time, in a different part of the world something positive was happening. South Africa that had one of the most brutal Apartheid regimes started to buckle under isolation and severe sanctions from the outside and the relentless internal violence. In a very quick space of time immense political changes took place in that country. One of the great personalities, Nelson Mandela, of the last 150 years was freed from prison to eventually take charge of his nation. History is amazing as we recount so many feuds and conflicts , every now and then some events do take place that renew one's faith in humanity and the power of peaceful dialogue. South Africa has not had an easy road pos-apartheid but at least every citizen of the country has an equal chance to live and share the good times as well the bad times.

At that time great changes had taken place around the world, the collapse of the Berlin Wall and the re-unification of Germany brought down the most potent symbols of the Soviet regime, Apartheid had ended in South Africa. The US and allies attacked Iraq and very quickly liberated Kuwait but decided not to topple Saddam Hussein.  Iran was pre-occupied by its internal troubles and faced economic pressures at home. Were we heading for a peaceful period? NO

Yugoslavia one of the many countries which were a part of the Soviet bloc had for some time had been distancing itself from the communist bloc then faced some major internal conflicts. The country had been formed through combining several states each one with its own national identity and in the case of Bosnia Herzegovina, a different religion. Some say this was a small massacre and cannot be termed as a genocide but what the Serb forces did to Bosnian Muslims and Bosnian Croats was most shameful and consisted of mass murder, rape in the most cruel manner. The culpable forces termed it as ethnic cleansing and how this could have happened in Europe right under the eyes of the so called Civilized world is hard to imagine. This will remain a dark chapter in the recent history for mankind to remember and make sure it is never allowed to happen again.

The events as mentioned affected every human's life in one way or another. The impact on ordinary people is profound. It may only be that they end paying more for petrol or the check in formalities for travel take a bit longer or some have family involved in the unfortunate conflicts and to the extent some become direct victims of the violence.

The above events created instability in the whole of the Middle East and with the events in Iran and Iraq heightened the tensions between the Shia and Sunni factions in Muslim countries. Many extreme Islamist organizations were formed such as Al Qaeeda. It was only a matter of time that these conflicts would spill over.

The great tragedy of 9/11 happened and the world changed forever. The perception of the world towards Muslims changed in the most negative way. Average people started to hate Muslims and the religion of Islam. The so called defenders of the faith who committed all these horrific acts destroyed the real image of Islam and what did they achieve? They set about to damage the USA termed as the great enemy but instead brought about misery for their own selves and their fellow brethren.

The US and the West invaded Iraq and Afghanistan without any conclusive results. Both countries remain unstable, suffer from internal violence. Further, terrorist groups have sprung up spreading hate and violence e.g ISIS, Boko Haram etc. There have been many regime changes in the the Middle East e.g. Egypt, Libya, Yemen etc and ongoing turmoil in Syria, Sudan. The world remains tense and wary of the terrorists.

Another positive thing happened along the line, the citizens of the USA elected a half American African person as their President. This was most unimaginable some 35 years ago when the country was unwilling to allow full freedom rights to the same group of people. President Obama served two terms without any major controversy.

USA has elected Mr.Donald Trump as its 45<sup>th</sup> President. I would give him time before passing judgement on him as a person or as a President. One thing for sure is that he loves his country.

# TECHNOLOGICAL DEVELOPMENTS IN THE LAST 65 YEARS

…..Technology made large populations possible; large populations now make technology indispensable. - Joseph Krutch (Writer)

To say that the technological developments in the last 70 years or so have been phenomenal would be an understatement many words come to mind as one tries to capture the essence of the developments and achievements e.g. remarkable, extraordinary, prodigious, astonishing, astounding etc. Sometimes when I hold my Mobile phone, I cannot believe that there in my hand is my complete office! The pace of technological development in my lifetime has been simply staggering.

Technological developments do have an impact on our life but this varies for each individual. One has to admire the human capability in how great minds have come up with some of the technological innovations most of which are making the modern day life that bit easier to live and at the same time increasing the efficiency of the cumulative Global output.

When I commenced life and from the age that I started to remember, I have seen some incredible changes which would have been beyond imagination for all people in my environment. I spent my early years in Hospital quarters for staff, these were powered by DC power!! And for a long while all appliances had to be capable of DC and AC operation. Telephones existed but all numbers had to be connected by calling the Operator

Some of these technological developments in the latest Weapons, machines, armaments, nuclear stock piles are the dooms day tools but we have to live with these all around us and some even pointed at us. In an ideal world these would not be needed but we live in a World full of conflict and tension. While there is a major R&D effort in development of these weapons of mass destruction and unimaginable capabilities the overall level of different technologies can be diverted for things which benefit mankind.

On the other hand the advances in medicine e.g. retrovial drugs to give Aids sufferers a chance , Various Cancer treatments , Heart transplants , advances  in medicines to help the ageing population of the world etc. all have contributed to more healthy and extended lives of people. Some dangerous diseases like Yellow fever and malaria have almost been eradicated. Every human has a better chance to live longer and enjoy a healthier life.  Hopefully, in time the medical advances will reach the very poor parts of the world and reduce human suffering.

The readers might say, why should they read the most obvious fact already known and repeated many times by so many. Please bear with me this compilation is to offer a different perspective on different things that impact the life of ordinary people like myself. This is our book and hope it will get the non − ordinary people to look at us in a different way.

There have been so many innovations and technological developments in my lifetime that it would not be possible to cover all of these. I will try and pick some that, I believe have been the most outstanding.

MEDICNE

Mention has been made of the developments in medicine be it Penicilin, Anti-biotics or other Vaccines to avoid serious disease are blessings. However, to have treatments available for diseases like Cancer and Aids which were hard to imagine only a couple of decades ago are indeed very remarkable. Hopefully these will become readily available in the near future to the real sufferers on the lower rung of economic power. Many of the diseases previously considered deadly have almost been eliminated e.g. Malaria, small pox etc. From time to time there are outbreaks of deadly viruses hitherto unknown but the guardians of modern medicine always find cure and long may this continue. For the invasive part of medicine great advances have been made to resolve issues with ailing hearts , liver , kidneys and other vital organs e.g. eyes. Plastic surgery gives human a chance and hope in case of some unfortunate event other than that this offers cosmetic options to those who want changes to their features and self and this part of medicine can produce some fascinating results. Further research in Stem Cells and human cloning are threatening new frontiers. The area that remains controversial is the use of artificial insemination. Undoubtedly, in some instances it provides hope and fulfillment but the overall concept is a subject of fierce debate and I shall reserve my judgment on the subject.

Although research on DNA was first completed in 1953, it did not become a major subject until a couple of decades ago. It has made great contributions in terms of DNA profiling and Genetic Engineering.

SPACE TRAVEL AND EXPLORATION

After the Second World War both the USA and the USSR set about racing each other to conquer space. There is no such thing as being able to conquer the vast unknown out and up there. However, incredible steps have been taken to enter the space and slowly but surely human beings will get to know what lies beyond. A great many technological leaps in Telecommunications have been possible by having Satellites orbiting the earth. Many of the mankind's daily chores and welfare depends upon this Satellite communication.

*It was in 1957, when the Soviet won the race to enter space by launching the Sputnik spacecraft which left the earth's atmosphere and orbited earth a few times and landed safely. The astronaut Yuri Gargan became the first man in space and definitely will remain an immortal hero.*

*The USA landed man on the moon in 1969, almost an impossible feat given that the technology then was not what it is today. This feat was repeated a few more times and in my opinion these achievements in outer space have to be considered even more extraordinary than others. To travel millions of miles in the dark unknown space, land on a planet with a harsh environment and then return is simply unbelievable.*

*Many space programs followed. The US pursued the Space shuttle projects to orbit the earth and carry out R&D in space and also with the capability to fly back after entering the stratosphere and land like any other aircraft.*

The USSR launched Space stations as a sort of permanent base in outer space to carry out useful experiments for the benefit of future mankind. Happily, as the

Cold war was coming to an end mutual co-operation for maintaining and manning at least one Space station has become a reality.

Many Communication Satellites have been launched in Space and continually orbit the earth for different interest groups. The combined effort of the European Countries has been the mainstay of many satellite launches using the US or the Russian capabilities in this area.

Lately, China and India have both achieved great successes with their space programs. China has put an unmanned spacecraft on the moon about a decade ago. India has actually succeeded in putting a space craft on the planet Mars. Both countries regularly launch Commercial satellites in Space.

DEVELOPMENT OF COMMERCIAL AIRCRAFTS

Everyone repeats the cliché that the world has become smaller and distances have become meaningless. The only reason this has happened is due to the advances in the type of Commercial aircraft that take to the skies. Ever since the de-regulation of the industry in the 70s where the Governments had no control over the air fares , air travel has boomed and the number of travellers and destinations has increased at an exponential rate.

All this has been made possible by the continuous development of the aircraft used in Commercial aviation. The speed, the comfort and Safety are important features of this industry. The statistics indicate excellent Safety records and the constant competition encourages developments on the technical and aesthetic features of the aircraft.

MICROPROCESSORS

The text book definition:

A microprocessor incorporates the functions of a CPU on a single integrated circuit or a few integrated circuits. It is a computer processor on a microchip and is a multipurpose, programmable device that uses digital data as input and provides results as an output once it processes the input according to instructions stored in its memory.

The development of microprocessors which entails one or two chips containing sufficient circuits to provide the Central Processing unit of a Computer is a concept even hard enough to fully comprehend for an Engineer like me. Rather than trying to analyze too much we must recognize this innovation as a marvel and appreciate the impact it has on every aspect of our life.

The pioneering work took place in the Silicon Valley and that is where the early models of the microprocessors were launched commercially. There is some doubt as to who actually invented the Microprocessor whether it was a team based at the giant Intel or an individual, Ted Hoff who first came up with the concept and a simple unit in the late 60s?

INTERNET

The inter connection of the Global computers and networks is another innovation with a direct impact on the modern day life. From the early work funded by the US Government in the 60s this global link became very popular from around the mid-90s. Currently, 50% of the global population are users and in developed countries with easier access to computers and networks this figure is closer to 81%.

MOBILE/SMART PHONES

In a few decades the whole concept and development of communication has changed at mega exponential rates. From using telephone calls connected by operators and telegrams, moving to telexes and on to digital phones and faxes followed by E-mails. All we need now is a smart phone to communicate verbally, pass data and arrange transactions in the far corners of the world. In places where there was no hope of getting networks and land lines for years to come the use of smart phones has brought about astonishing changes to the lives of the population concerned.

Both of the above innovations have social stigma and a negative aspects through abuse and in the case of latter the safety of drivers using mobile phones.

## ROBOTS AND ARTIFICAL INTELLIGENCE

There are many mega innovations at different stage of Research and development and all will have an impact on the lives of each aspect of this world that we live in.

The one that catches the attention is the advent of Robots and Artificial Intelligence. Somewhat of a spooky prospect!

Like the term "robot" itself, artificial intelligence is hard to define. Ultimate AI would be a recreation of the human thought process -- a man-made machine with our intellectual abilities. This would include the ability to learn just about anything, the ability to reason, the ability to use language and the ability to formulate original ideas.

# THE 'GREAT' BRITAIN OR THE UNITED KINGDOM

……."He stood staring into the wood for a minute, then said: "What is it about the English countryside — why is the beauty so much more than visual? Why does it touch one so?" anon

THE UNITED KINGDOM

The only real democracy in the world with a Parliament over 300 years old. Everyone has a right and a say in this country. The system is set up to look after the sick and the old and those less unfortunate have financial support available under the Welfare system. The true democracy leads to the extremists too having a say and that is when some unlawful acts occur threatening the well-being and sometimes even the lives of the rest of the citizens. The Welfare system is abused extensively but overall it benefits the people who deserve it the most. The Education system is one of the oldest and the best in the world. UK has some of the leading educational institutions in the world. The government has had to adopt its policies to accept many other races and religions and it has done so and is doing so from the grass root levels. UK has been criticized for not doing enough on this count, in my opinion they were a bit late in initiating the various initiatives but now are well on the way. The Police force is one of the most effective and most of the officers still do not carry firearms. Judiciary is powerful and independent. The Civil Service is the best in the world even though the subject of some ridicule over their apparent discipline and inflexibility.

This is a truly civilized country. I am very proud to be British for so many different reasons. This is not just a statement but a passionate declaration. I recall that during the summer Olympics of 2012 in London, a group of UK expatriates including me were watching some of the events on the TV. We were at one stage watching Jessica Ennis wrap up the Gold medal and naturally all were enjoying the moment. Her beaming smile brought a lump to everyone's throat. Later on over some drinks, a British gentleman came over to me and said that he was watching me during the event and he felt that by watching the emotion and my body language he was convinced that I loved the UK. He had never seen this kind of passion coming from someone who had not been born in the UK and was a non-white. In spite of the brusque comment I took it as a compliment.

Having established that it is my country and it is where my future grandchildren will grow and be good citizens, we have to move on. At this current moment when Theresa May has just triggered the article 50 for BREXIT. I feel that this is a wrong move for the future of the UK and its people. The nation is divided on this issue and the majority (a slim one) has voted to leave the European Community largely based on one fear the rising number of immigrants. Sadly, the fact is that overall immigration numbers are not likely to reduce by much just the identity and origin of the immigrants will change. The UK will create many burdens for itself. Securing trade deals with Europe will not be a cake walk because in order to deliver a stiff message to any other likely EXITERS the EU will be mean and tough. Then there is the financial bill of around Eu 50 bn to be paid. Divestments instead of further investments from global businesses, who located here to build bridge heads into Europe are more than likely. Certainly the Foreign Car manufacturer's withdrawal could hurt the British Economy very hard. More burden is being created for HM Customs and Excise department. It is felt a favourable Trade deal with USA will be granted? Is that really going to happen? When the US President has openly stated that all future Trade deals will be in favour of only USA. The so called other potential markets of the Commonwealth have their own agendas. First of all the buying power of most of the Commonwealth countries is limited. Even the most prosperous ones see the UK Products and Services as the premium end of the market and there is hesitation to give priority to these offerings. Are we really going to get favourable Trade deals with China and India? As someone who has been involved in International marketing for a very long time, I hereby voice my humble opinion that UK Overseas Trade faces unprecedented challenges for years to come. UK industry has fought over the years to become competitive and efficient at some cost to the employment situation. I am afraid more of the same is required for a few more years to be able to fit in the new scenario.  I do not believe the vested interests of parties and politicians who backed the BREXIT campaign put issues like immigration and nationalism ahead of reality. None of the so called Brexit leaders like Boris Johnson, Nigel Farage etc really had a plan to go forward with Brexit. They orchestrated less than honest rhetoric playing on people's fears and sadly they succeeded.

I am a Royalist and in spite of the negative news over the last two decades H.M the Queen brings distinction to the country and it adds glory and pomp to the nation. Having lived as an expatriate in Malaysia, I have had the Honour to be one of the many to meet with her Majesty during her visit to this country during the Commonwealth games of 1998. Since then some of the other Royals have visited Malaysia on official visits. I can safely say that some of them are not my most favourite people. I would say the lineage will survive as the heir and grandson of H.M the Queen, Prince William and his wife Kate have the charisma to carry the role well into the future.

Looking back over the years, since the end of the World War 2, the political and social scenario has changed in ways that no one could have imagined. Many expert views and analysis have been written on the subject. Here are the views in very simple words.

In a total of 72 years since the end of the war, GB has been ruled for 45 years by the Conservatives and 30 years by the Labour party. It has to be said that the best economic periods have mostly been under the rule of the Conservative party. Although the period 1997 – 2010 and especially under the leadership of Tony Blair till 2007, there were periods of prosperity. Peace was finally brought to Northern Ireland. Then again, Tony Blair had given up the hard core values of the Labour party and had moved to the Centre and even the Conservatives admired him.

1946-51

Of course Labour Party set up the Welfare State and the National Health Service straight after coming to power at the end of the War. They also nationalized the major Industrial and financial institutions. Overall, after the end of war they were responsible for arresting the decline of the wellbeing and health of the people. In that period the party oversaw the granting of independence to many of the former colonies, a process which continued under the Conservatives well into the

60s. Labour also had to re-build the Finances of the country and they did a reasonable job after receiving soft loans and grants from the USA and Canada.

1951- 1964

In early 50s the Conservatives got into power and started a prolonged rule for 13 years. In that period GB set itself as a dominant world power and took the centre stage in some of the major issues and conflicts of the world e.g The Korean war, The Suez Canal etc. with better economic conditions GB needed additional human resources and that started the non-white immigration from the former colonies. Finally, due unpopular economic policies the Conservatives lost power and it did not help that the foreign secretary Lord Profumo was found sharing a mistress with the a diplomat at the Russian Embassy!

While President De Gaulle of France lived there was no chance of GB becoming a member of the European Union. He did not approve of the close relation that GB had with the USA

1964-1970

Labour returned to power under Harold Wilson .In that period the Trade Unions gained excessive Power and problems started to surface due to too much of nationalization. The Pound was devalued in 1967 which was a very unpopular move at that time.  This was a period of low unemployment and a period of relative prosperity. Wilson introduced many Socialist Liberal policies which came to the fore under the Social Changes to the GB

Later under his stint country started to suffer from High inflation and the rising unemployment

1970 -1974

The Conservatives returned to Power with Edward Heath as the Prime Minister. The growing power of the Trade Unions resulted in the Strike Culture and the country suffered as a direct result of this. Immigration of the non –whites started to become a major political issue. In 1973, after the Arab – Israel war the first of the Oil Shocks resulted with a sharp rise in Prices due to the strong emergence of

OPEC. The people of GB were reeling from this when the Miners went on strike reducing the country to a three day working week and scheduled power cuts.

Edward Heath did negotiate the entry of GB into the European Economic Community. At that time De Gaulle had lost power.

During his tenure the unemployment was controlled and a brief period of economic upturn was experienced

Also, the decimalization of the Currency came into being and it was a goodbye to the Shillings and the Farthings.

1974 – 1979

Labour returned to power with Wilson as PM and he quit after two years allowing Callaghan to take charge. There were conspiracy theories attached to Wilson's unexpected departure ranging from being complicit in a Soviet Union plot to topple democracy in GB to him being a KGB spy. Most of the theories have been officially rejected and closed. The official explanation was that these stories were planted by MI5 to discredit Wilson.

However, this period under Labour was definitely not good for the Britons. Wilson went for a referendum in the house to decide whether to stay within the European Economic Community or not on 5th June 1975 and won the vote to stay.

The inflation levels rose to highs of up to 27% and the unemployment was up to 1.5m or 10% of the workforce

Callaghan suffered a crushing defeat in the summer of 1979.

1979 -1997

The conservatives ruled GB in a very significant period for the country. Margaret Thatcher who came to power in May 1979 till she was pushed out in Nov 1990 was the main protagonist and undoubtedly one of the greatest Prime Ministers of GB. Through a series of bold policies she changed GB forever. She is accredited with the following

- At the risk of allowing first for un-employment which peaked at 3.1 m people in 1982 her economic policies eventually brought prosperity. She brought inflation down to single figures from a peak of 27% during the Labour regime

- Financial de-regulation, de-nationalization of state assets and creating an environment for entrepreneurship

- Literally destroyed the Trade Union Power

- Took GB to a successful war against Argentina some 2000 miles away in the Atlantic Ocean to re-occupy the Falklands

- Sowing the seeds for the eventual peace deal in Northern Ireland

- Taking a defining role in close co-operation with President Reagan of the USA to end the Cold War with the demise of the Soviet Union.

- She was never warm to the concept of a complete European Economic and Monetary Union. She believed that the role of the EC should be limited to ensuring free trade and effective competition and not much more. However, she was convinced by her Senior Ministers to sign up to the European Exchange Rate Mechanism in October 1990. Her stance on the wider EC Union made her very unpopular with some of her Key Minsters and combined with the declining economic conditions and her obsession and insistence upon an unpopular local tax brought her downfall within the Conservative Party.

John Major was elected the Party Leader and became the new PM. He was the grey man of GB politics but had to oversee some major events in his tenure. He did call for General election in the spring of 1992 and against many odds retained the power with a slim majority. He had to oversee the first Gulf War.

However, one of the most eventful days of his tenure fell on the 16th September 1992. As GB had signed up for the ERM then they had to ensure that the depreciating Sterling had to be defended with the reserves to honour the terms of the treaty. The UK government attempted to prop up the depreciating pound to avoid withdrawal from the monetary system the country had joined two years earlier. John Major raised interest rates to 10 percent and authorized the spending of billions worth of foreign currency reserves to buy up the sterling being sold on the currency markets but the measures failed to prevent the pound falling below its minimum level in the ERM. The Treasury took the decision to defend the sterling's position, believing that to devalue would be to promote inflation.

Soros' Quantum Fund began a massive sell-off of pounds on Tuesday, 15 September 1992. The Exchange Rate Mechanism stated that the Bank of England was required to accept any offers to sell pounds. However, the Bank of England only accepted orders during the trading day. When the markets opened in London the next morning, the Bank of England began their attempt to prop up their currency as per the decision made by Norman Lamont and Robin Leigh-Pemberton, the then Chancellor of the Exchequer and Governor of the Bank of England respectively. They began buying orders to the amount of 300 million pounds twice before 8:30 AM to little effect. The Bank of England's intervention was ineffective because Soros' Quantum Fund was dumping pounds far faster. The Bank of England continued to buy and Quantum continued to sell until Lamont told Prime Minister John Major that their pound purchasing was failing to produce results.

At 10:30 AM on 16 September, the British government announced a rise in the base interest rate from an already high 10 to 12 percent to tempt speculators to buy pounds. Despite this and a promise later the same day to raise base rates again to 15 percent, dealers kept selling pounds, convinced that the government would not stick with its promise. By 7:00 that evening, Norman Lamont, then Chancellor, announced Britain would leave the ERM and rates would remain at the new level of 12 percent; however, on the next day interest rate was back on 10%. It was later revealed that the decision to withdraw had been agreed at an emergency meeting during the day between Norman Lamont, Prime Minister John Major, Foreign Secretary Douglas Hurd, President of the Board of Trade Michael Heseltine, and Home Secretary Kenneth Clarke (the latter three all being staunch pro-Europeans as well as senior Cabinet Ministers), and that the interest rate hike to 15% had only been a temporary measure to prevent a rout in the pound that afternoon.

On a personal level, I remember very clearly that morning I was invited in by the MD of the company that I worked for and was advised that as a result of my previous efforts I had been appointed as the Sales Director of an export orientated SME. The company manufactured Precision Instruments for Machine Tools and exported 90% of its product worldwide, USA being the largest market. The news was of great delight and satisfaction to me but rather than celebrate I had to attend to a delegation of very important customers on a visit to the UK from Singapore. Thus, my attention was not so focused on being a good host but escaping the meetings repeatedly to check the news as there was no Internet in those days. By mid-morning the Sterling value had stregthened substantially against the US Dollar and I knew full well that would mean serious difficulties in meeting targets as Exports especially to US would be hit. I had arranged Lunch with my visitors in Stratford upon Avon followed by a barge trip to introduce the guests to the world of Shakespeare. By the time I got on the barge the interest rates had been raised to 15% but the Sterling was still strengthening. At that stage , I thought that perhaps this appointment would be the most short lived of my career and in fact at those kind of interest rates and the Currency exchange rate the company would not survive either. So I toasted myself with a glass of DRY white wine.

However, by the time we returned to the hotel in the evening, Britain had pulled out of the ERM. The interest rates started to ease and the Sterling started to stabilize. I had been to hell and back in one day.

Returning to John Major's leadership , he espoused Back to the Basics and family values thus when a few years later it was revealed that he was having an affair with a controversial Cabinet Minister Edwina Currie it sort of put paid to his honest man image. Some even gave him credit for his indiscretions on the basis that he was not the grey man everyone imagined him to be.

1997 – 2010

Finally, Labour got into power and had a 13 year run. Tony Blair became Prime Minister under the new Labour banner in which he brought them to the centre of the political spectrum.  Through reformist policies he oversaw a sustained period of economic growth. He brought about partial devolution to Scotland and Wales setting up regional Parliaments. He had a strong Chancellor in Gordon Brown who was popular with the financial community. He led Labour to three election Victories and seemed to have to all but weakened the Conservative party forever.

The long-running Northern Ireland peace process was brought to a conclusion in 1998 with the Belfast Agreement which established a devolved Northern Ireland Assembly and de-escalated the violence associated with the problems.

Tony Blair was criticized for his total commitment to G W Bush and his policies on the Middle East and the second Gulf war and the military action in Afghanistan.

The Government was also criticized for the lax policies on Immigration especially from within the European Union.

Tony Blair handed the power to Gordon Brown in June 2007 as that was the understanding the two had reached some years earlier and had not had a formal leadership contest for the unity of the party. From Gordon Brown's point of view this may have not been the best time to take charge after ten years of one party rule it was natural that their popularity was sinking. However, being a good Economist he handled the severe economic crisis of 2008 better than the other European counterparts. He delayed calling for the General Election to get his mandate directly from the people and even his party criticized him for that.

General Election was held in May 2010 and Britain ended with a hung parliament. Conservatives had the narrow majority and they made a deal with the Liberal Democrats to form a Coalition government.

2010 –

David Cameroon became the Prime Minister. He started to bring back Thatcherite economic policies by increasing indirect taxation and reducing Government spending in attempt to reduce the rising budget deficit. On international affairs he maintained GB's stance over the Middle East and Afghanistan.

A Scottish referendum in October 2014 for them to gain independence was rejected giving the Government a stronger position.

As the economic situation became better, David Cameroon was able to win the election of 2015 with a clear majority and the Conservatives were back in a strong political position.

As a part of his election manifesto, David Cameroon had agreed to a national Referendum on whether to stay in the EU or not. On June 23rd, 2016 Britain voted for the Brexit leading to his resignation.

Teresa May was elected the Party Leader and hence the Prime Minister


Decline of Manufacturing Skills

During and after the Second World War, Great Britain had arguably had the best manufacturing skills than any other developed nations. I personally believe that the manufacturing skills and the discipline of that generation played a huge part in the eventual victory during the World War II. I worked in the British industry and remained in awe of the skills, the dedication of the majority of the workers. Thus, it was sad to see these virtues being eroded first by the Trade Union disruptions and later on the inability to remain competitive causing a shift away from manufacturing. I say it with conviction that if a nation does not have a large manufacturing base it will always have issues with unemployment. These set of skills also started to disappear as the successive Governments put in little emphasis on craft or vocational training. Industry cut down on Training expenditures and the younger generation showed less interest in the 'dirty' world of manufacturing instead opting for the more glamorous Service sector.

UK manufacturing has been in relative decline since the 1960s. Manufacturing as a share of real GDP has fallen from 32% in 1970 to 12% in 2010.

Firstly, the percentage of jobs in manufacturing and industrial production has steadily declined. In the late 60s 42% of jobs were in manufacturing, by 1980, 25%. By 2010, the percentage of jobs in manufacturing had fallen to 8.2%.

Great Britain like many other countries went through recessions in 1974, 1981, 1991 and 2008-09. In all of these periods there was a drastic fall in output and the unemployment levels rose. However, each time the labour productivity increased substantially as a result of enforced cutback on resources employed.

Reasons for relative decline in manufacturing


Fall in relative productivity. Manufacturing is traditionally an important export sector. Relative wage costs and productivity are very important for determining demand and competitiveness. The UK has struggled to remain competitive with lower wage cost economies, like China. However, it is a myth to suggest manufacturing labour productivity has been falling. A study of British manufacturing suggests labour productivity rose 50% between 1997 and 2007. (Price Waterhouse & Cooper)

 Manufacturing is export led, the sector is quite sensitive to changes in the Global exchange rates. The periods of the strongest declines in  GB manufacturing occurred during periods of a strong Sterling, e.g. in early 1980s, and early 2000s However ,the strong Sterling in the period 2000-2007, perhaps held back growth of manufacturing. However, the strong Sterling theory doesn't explain the long term decline. There is evidence that a deep recession can lead to a permanent loss of output and the damage is permanent. It is also worth noting the fall in the Sterling post 2008 has done little to boost growth.

Thus the relatively high unemployment is here to stay for the foreseeable future.


Another major change in the Social landscape of the country which creates a serious issue that GB is now a multi –faith country. Years of immigration have resulted in significant number of Muslims, Hindus, Buddhists and Sikhs becoming members of the society. The most visible religious minority are the Muslims and whether it is admitted or not there is serious concern amongst the indigenous population given the perceived association of this community with violence and practices which cause concern.

| Census Year | Number of Muslims | Population of England & Wales | % of population | Number of registered mosques |
|---|---|---|---|---|
| 1961 | 50,000 | 46,196,000 | 0.11% | 7 |
| 1971 | 226,000 | 49,152,000 | 0.46% | 30 |
| 1981 | 553,000 | 49,634,000 | 1.11% | 149 |
| 1991 | 950,000 | 51,099,000 | 1.86% | 443 |
| 2001 | 1,600,000 | 52,042,000 | 3.07% | 614 |
| 2011 | 2,706,000 | 56,076,000 | 4.83% | 1,500 |

RACE RELATIONS

The British Government and the NGOs have done a lot to bring an end to racism. Things are much better, there are many laws to protect the minority victims. Sadly, Great Britain has a wide element of racists in every segment of society but more pronounced and vocal in the lower classes. These people would think nothing of abusing or causing physical hurt to people of a different colour of skin or of a different faith. In addition there is a sinister Right Wing element backed by the rich and powerful who have their profound ugly agenda to undermine and if possible eliminate the dark skinned people. Much as I am proud of my country, I have to acknowledge that this attitude does exist in the society and perhaps will never be eliminated.

LIVING IN GREAT BRITAIN

As I have mentioned elsewhere in the book that I never felt uncomfortable living in the different parts of the country. I still enjoy my regular visits back to United Kingdom. There is nothing like going to a traditional pub and having a 'ploughman's lunch with a pint or two of real ale. It also helps to have a real sense of humour where you can take jokes as well as crack them. One must also not be too sensitive as the British crack jokes about each other i.e. English ridicule Scots, Irish and the Welsh and the compliment is returned with interest. Of course the British really have a go at the Germans, the French and the Americans. Naturally the Pakistanis and Indians also have to receive their share along with the Black community. Of course there is a line between having harmless fun to when it becomes nasty and hurtful. Normally, the British people will crack innocent jokes to break the ice. One thing is for sure that if a person does not have a sense of humour then they are not going to enjoy life in the United Kingdom.

While we are at it for the benefit of non-British readers:

Great Britain is: England, Wales, and Scotland

United Kingdom is: Great Britain and Northern Ireland

I have lived in many places in Great Britain and everywhere had its own charm. One thing is for sure when you enter your home in that country and draw your curtains you feel safe and secure. You are indeed in your castle and you feel protected as the whole system is geared to look after you.

I enjoyed living in rural Lincolnshire just outside the city in a small village known as washing borough. The Community spirit is great in such places and everyone gets to know everyone. All the necessary amenities are there like a GP surgery , Garage and Petrol Shop , small shopping Centre , traditional Butcher's shop , Hair dresser , Fish and Chips outlet and of course a couple of pubs. In addition there is the Community Centre, Nursery for younger children and a Primary school. There are always plenty of playing fields and the local Football, Rugby, Cricket and Bowls clubs. The result is a very stable and simple life especially if you have a young family. Of course if one wanted real action the place is not far from bigger cities like Nottingham and Leicester and London is only one hour away from the nearby Newark Railway station. The myth that English are unfriendly and stiff upper lipped and neighbours take no interest are perhaps true in some areas of the country but by and large there is extensive interaction but no intrusion in each other's life. Of course living in the bigger cities is a lot different and due to the overcrowding social and cultural problems creep in. It is a sad fact that the income levels dictate the neighbourhood that one lives in and hence invariably the less skilled and less well-off immigrants end up in the very deprived areas of the inner cities. They then have to compete with the less well off from the host community for the limited benefits available and that is how the serious problems arise.

I had the privilege of living in Aberdeen, Scotland and I cherish that period on account of the great scenic beauty that was around me and the gracious hospitality of the Scots.It is already mentioned elsewhere in the book that the myth that Scots are stingy is totally false. I cannot understand how this myth was created but I enjoyed my time in Scotland and the people were always very warm. Of course the larger cities like Glasgow and Edinburgh have their own sets of social problems as other inner cities in the UK.

I lived in Liverpool in the late sixties and early seventies it was a very bad period for that city due to the virtual wipeout of the docks and the historical Port. Sadly there was depravation and poverty due to high unemployment. The people of Liverpool fondly called Scousers maintained their sense of humour for a very long time, almost two decades before relative economic stability brought about the rejuvenation of the city.

It is fun to live in the UK because there are so many different type of places to visit. There are so many historical places that capture one's imagination. Whether the Robin Hood legend is true or not there is a definitely a Sherwood Forest and the Castle of the Sheriff of Nottingham.

The Dales in Yorkshire are unique and consist of beautiful adulating countryside a drive through some of these brings one in close contact with the true English character. Everywhere there are ample pubs offering comfortable and wholesome Bed and Breakfast packages.

The cities of Bath and Lincoln provide remnants of the Roman presence in this land.

Wales is a beautiful part of the UK and there are unique places to visit as illustrated below.

One of the most interesting place to visit and actually considered a Wonder of the World is Stonehenge.

There are many historic Castles and Cathedrals dotted across the country reflecting the various periods of the history.

The South West of the country all the way to the Land's end is different to the rest of the country with relatively less dense population and clean air . Beautiful sprawling coastal towns and villages are wonderful retreats.


LONELY PLANET – GREAT BRITAIN

This is a great Country to visit with it History, Architectural magnificence, Traditions, Royalty and sheer Physical beauty.

UK is also the Global Centre of Arts, Fashion & Style, Music

I can only recommend some of the most outstanding sights and places but there is a great deal to see and enjoy in this GREAT country.

Pictures tell a story in a more powerful way than words, so I will try to tempt you all with a few selected ones.


LONDON – Undoubtedly the most exciting City in the world. It has something for everyone.

MOST RECOGNIZABLE VIEW OF LONDON

WINDSOR CASTLE

WHITE CLIFFS OF DOVER

BATH

DEVON

DORSET

THE STONE HENGE

CORNWALL

UNIVERSITY CITY OF OXFORD

AND CAMBRIDGE

STRATFORD UPON AVON

WARWICK CASTLE

THE PEAK DISTRICT – DERBYSHIRE

NOTTINGHAMSHIRE – THE SHERWOOD FOREST

SNOWDONIA NATIONAL PARK - WALES

# PORTMOEIRIN – WALES

CONWY- WALES

THE YORKSHIRE MOORS

YORK

THE LAKE DISTRICT

HADRIAN'S WALL

GLASGOW – LOCH LOMOND

TRUSSACHS

EDINBURGH

## THE ROYAL DEESIDE

## GLENEAGLES

# LOCHNESS

# THE WORKING LIFE

**..........Success is no accident. It is hard work, perseverance, learning, studying, sacrifice and most of all, love of what you are doing or learning to do.   Pele**

Those of us who are not born into wealth have to work to survive and lucky are those who actually end up doing what they enjoy. The worst thing in life must be to work hard doing something that one does not enjoy but has no choice but to persevere for survival. Such an unhappy situation can destroy the soul of a person. In the past many people ended up in the wrong jobs and situations largely because there was no career guidance, skill and ability matching or the many psychometric types of tests which can highlight individual strengths and weaknesses.

Trillions of books and papers have been written by the leading and the learned people on the Work related subjects. The career patterns are fast moving even to the extent that it is impossible to keep up with the pace of job descriptions. Entrepreneurs make their own rules and write their own books.

There is no doubt the traditional view of work and a job has changed forever. With the imminent arrival of the 4$^{th}$ Industrial Revolution and the Cyber Physical Systems the forecast is for a reduction in 20 years of up to 50% of the current jobs! There are more people than jobs in the new order and in the mature economies of Western Europe in particular the level of unemployment amongst the displaced highly qualified /experienced and fresh graduates is disproportionally high. The security that the 'job' offered has gone and people are left to fend for themselves. It is very tough for people if they have been in a job for a number of years and due to some change in circumstances their career gets de-railed. To rebuild their career takes a while and a serious endeavour is required with no guarantee of achieving previous level of. This is a sad fact and has many social implications in terms of family life. Fresh graduates also have a tough time, the one's who secure jobs are the lucky one's. A lot of these new additions to the job market struggle and some get disillusioned and go towards doing something well below their capabilities. This to me is a waste of human Capital.

Of course some of the new comers to the job market with entrepreneurial talent will find a way to succeed and do better on their own as compared to what they might have achieved working for someone else. Entrepreneurs make their own rules and write their own books.

There are always exceptions to the evolving pattern and that makes for an easier passage and a happy ending for at least some people.

If people are lucky enough to sustain a career in terms of full time employment then the next phase is to seek elevation in the career ladder to go right to the top. This of course means competition fair or unfair to fulfil career ambitions and take the top positions and become senior executives and indeed leaders.

FACTORS THAT MAKE A SUCCESSFUL BUSINESS LEADER/MANAGER

- There is no substitute for hard work. The most successful leaders/managers are always the hardest working people. Taking that extra step makes a difference. In my own case, I felt that I did not take that extra step when the situations arose in my working life, highlighting a sub conscious lack of effort.
- The strength and the pedigree of the character shape the level of professionalism in Business managers.
- Self-motivation and discipline are essential ingredients
- Entrepreneurial flair is an ability and a gift that very few have. The ability to spot an opportunity and then take it forward to embrace success and fortune is for the special few in this world. No amount of training or in depth study can attain this natural skill.
- Leaders are born with a multitude of skills and abilities e.g. charisma, vision, entrepreneurial flair, calmness in adversity etc.
- Managers can also be trained to be leaders of sorts but this type will never match the natural born leaders.
- A stable personal life has a positive impact on achieving success. Having suffered an unstable marriage between the age of 34 to 44 impeded my career growth and many opportunities slipped by due to pre-occupation with an ugly domestic situation.
- Luck does play a part. Being in the right place at the right time does quicken the journey.
- Having a vision and a plan is a must and it is also important to totally believe in it and commit to it.
- Must have a good awareness of the overall environment and a grasp of the macro and micro Economic factors around one's self.

- Knowledge through experience helps in a sense of relevance
- Must have knowledge or flair for understanding 'numbers'. Familiarity with Accountancy and Cash Management is vital for success.
- Understanding the International business environment is critical given the globalization of business and this involves in becoming familiar with different cultures, customs, languages and geographical locations.
- Knowledge of the relevant sector is essential as more respect can be gained by demonstrating an ease and comfort with subjects being dealt with.

Each of the above statements can be a subject of Empirical Research by scholars involved in Business management studies.

If the scope of this text has to be defined and then I am only able to comment on my experiences as an Engineer fighting his way to survive in a very complex world. Not blessed with great intelligence or technical knowhow somehow I have survived 44 years and now it is easier to handle most situations in an Engineering environment. Perhaps some of the views based on a global experience may be useful to some readers and that is the main motive of fashioning this text.

I have always tended to be an autocratic leader and perhaps that does impact on effectiveness. I have mellowed over the years and learnt to listen and be more balanced in my approach. My personal belief is that the different styles of leadership and management are related to the working culture and the geographical location. Western style of management has little room for autocracy whereas the Asian practices are based on hard and disciplinarian style. Increasingly as the work environment becomes more skilled and complex the autocratic style of management will make way for new techniques and styles dictated by the rapid progress of technology and the ever changing work environment.

PERSONAL EXPERIENCE

I am the most impractical person even to the extent that all household repairs, changing plugs etc are handled by my wife. I was never meant to be an Engineer but that was long decided by my parents that since I could not be a Doctor of Medicine as they both were then I only had one choice. Years ago the career as a Doctor or an Engineer and perhaps a Lawyer were seen as the only options to achieve grandeur.

I made the most of the University life and somehow between excessive partying picked up useful information which did help me in the later years. University was followed by Industrial Training under my first Employer's Graduate program. At first this was a shock, the change in hours, discipline, dealing with different levels of intellect and learning new mechanical skills. At that time, I did not realize how privileged I was to have that opportunity of learning the basic Engineering skills which over the years have virtually disappeared.

There was no career advice on how to follow a path to become a Manager! I wanted to be something different and in a more elevated place than just being the Manager and wanted to be free of the factory environment. Since my Employer was one of the leading manufacturer of Industrial Gas Turbines largely serving the Oil and Gas Companies around the whole world, I could see my salvation in the opportunity to travel around the world.

I was never going to achieve my objectives by my level of technical knowledge. I was not going to succeed in the Sales and Marketing roles as those appointments for marketing capital intensive products were meant for the 'Gentlemen's Club' and my face and colour did not fit the bill. The other problem was that one had to be at least over 40 years of age to be taken seriously.

Since my background was in Electronics, I worked very hard to get the grasp of the Control Systems of the Industrial Gas Turbines and somehow managed to get appointed as a Product Training Instructor for World Wide clients who came to UK to improve their knowledge of the different Gas Turbines. I learnt a lot from meeting different sets of people each month and this gave me a meaningful insight into the worldwide Oil and Gas plants etc I also focussed on **learning some of the relevant languages** e.g. Spanish , French. Most of all I discovered that if I had a strength it was the **interpersonal skills and bridging**

**the gaps between different cultures**. Also being a part of the Training department I picked up a lot of information on the Mechanical and thermodynamic aspects of the Gas Turbines.

As I got on well with many of the visiting customers seeking product training, I was soon invited to visit their sites in different countries to conduct training courses. **I was on my way to achieving my objectives**. With the increasing knowledge of the whole of the Gas Turbine I was hauled into the Service/Commissioning department handling complex assignments around the globe. In time, I was in a position to be a team leader, my first attempt failed as I was too autocratic and inflexible. I had no management or supervisory training just my arrogance to believe I was good because all the customers liked me. I changed very quickly and tried to **learn from my superiors** especially from the one's that I liked and who I responded to better than the others. Although I have always remained a little bit autocratic but have learnt **about man management and flexibility**.

Next phase was assignments in varied locations such as Iran (pre-revolution), UAE, Saudi Arabia, North Africa, North Sea, Peru, Argentina, USA etc. That period built up the confidence to travel and handle a variety of challenges. The man management skills improved handling small teams. **Learnt a little bit of Costs vs Revenue**, **Resource allocation** etc in doing project management.

That led to a prestigious appointment to be seconded to British Petroleum in their Offices at Dyce, Aberdeen to play a leading role in the Maintenance of the equally famous Forties Off shore Fields. My company's Gas Turbines were the core of all activities in providing Power, in Pumping Crude oil and in compressing and transporting Gas. The maintenance of these Turbines was of a paramount importance and the responsibility was awesome. Apart from the technical pressures there was the concern on how I would get on with the hard

Scotsmen who formed the bulk of the Workforce and Management aboard the four Offshore Oil rigs in the Forties field. I got on very well with everyone and in fact I was treated with great respect and got to know the big hearted and generous Scots. **I developed strong PR skills in dealing with staff of a leading multi –national the secret was to back them up with intensity. The key to success was to have a total professional attitude.** This was a transitionary period from being just a 'maverick globe trotter' to being a mature Employee of the Company. I worked on other offshore installations such as the Shell Brent Field and Elf Norge Equitaine – on the Norwegian side but the period spent with BP on the Forties till to date remains a pinnacle of my career. Even almost forty years later within the Oil and Gas Industry this earns me respect to be recognized as a veteran of the North Sea. In terms of Technical knowledge **I learnt about the procedures in operating offshore platforms, the Health and Safety aspects, Survival knowledge in harsh conditions etc**

All the time the Commercial skills were developing but nothing could have prepared me for the next big challenge. I was appointed as the General Manager of a Joint Venture company in Mexico engaged in maintenance of gas Turbines and Plants. Some of the challenges ahead were:

- Spanish was the main language and within the context of the relevant work and customers the only workable option.

- Difficult Mexican JV partners who held the upper hand as it was their Country. On the other hand the UK business leaders who had a 49% stake but held the thing together thought they owned the business outright.

- Unbelievable Economic environment i.e. Inflation rate of 80% and daily devaluation of Mexican Peso vs US Dollars and hence all major currencies.

- Mexican employees who were temperamental at the best of times needed counselling to be motivated.

- Expatriate Employees who thought they were doing the company a favour by serving in Mexico.

- Awkward local bureaucratic officials who put up lots of barriers.

- One Colossal Customer that was the nation's pride throughout the history of Mexico i.e. Pemex the national Oil Company not known for its generosity to part owned or fully owned Foreign Vendors.

- Unusual natural phenomenas e.g. volcanic eruptions in the vicinity and massive Earthquakes.

I had to quickly learn about Financial and Management Accounting (a) to control the business and (b) to conform to the stringent financial reporting format for the UK principal.

I had to learn to deal with external Auditors and the preying internal accountants from the Head Office. Given the onerous challenge and the amount of effort needed on a daily basis I did not welcome the interference of the accountants and that turned out to be a big mistake.

I also swiftly learnt the most important lesson in my life CASH FLOW PLANNING. This was a tough one given the economic environment and the tightness of liquidity in the country and with no facilities with banks. Pemex were not know to pay earlier than 90 days. This was a lonely undertaking and no one really helped and each moment there was pressure to stay afloat. The end of the month was always a time of great stress.

In some ways Cash Flow good or bad was a fact but I had to deal with a daily devaluation of the Mexican Peso. For a business that had some of its costs posted in UK Sterling and most of the revenue was posted in the Peso. It was a dangerous balancing act because no one was prepared to take the risk and hedge.

I ran a successful business and in tough conditions and expanded four fold in a period of three years through extensive PR. To the Mexicans I was a rarity as I looked like them and almost spoke like them, yet I was not one of them. There is no business model for such a situation.

I battled hard as I could but the accountants at the HQ could not fathom out the Mexican Economy or its dynamics. Continuous pressure was ruining my health and that at the age of 35 with a young family those were good grounds to quit with honour.

What I had learnt in my time in Mexico was akin to a practical version of an MBA but I needed a formal acknowledgement. So, I enrolled for a Distance Learning MBA with Henley the Management College renowned for MBAs with International Business orientation. At the same time I took up an appointment with a Small Mechanical fabrication Company as the General Manager. The company was based in rural Lincolnshire and manufactured all types of Trailers and simple Agricultural Machinery. The company had been acquired by a larger and a very successful Agricultural retail group who needed to replace the outgoing (retiring) management and to bring the company up to date with the modern day realities. Most of the workforce was from the local rural area and I have to say that in my time with that company I never felt as a person of a different race. I was treated with great respect by all and judged on merit. I enjoyed the period and brought in new and innovative ideas. The reason I make this comment is to emphasize the fact that the location of the company was in a very rural area, population less than 500. One would imagine the local people in such a small place with no previous experience of dealing with people of another race to be a bit more defensive. Thus I have to re-state that in spite of the very serious issues with Race relations in the UK by and large the vast majority do give everyone a chance.

The owners of this business could not come to terms with the low profitability of a manufacturing business as compared to the higher margins for the Retail side that they were enjoying at that time. However, the manufacturing company that I dealt with changed its working culture and many of the new working practises even filtered through to the retail side as well.

 After about a year, I started to miss the International interface as after all that is what I had grown up with. Thus when an offer came to join another public listed holding Company with a diverse range of product portfolio to develop their business interests in the Far East, I jumped at the chance. This worked out very well for me as it lead to the journey which brought me to Malaysia and so many of the chapters of this book narrate the different experiences along the way.

I did complete my MBA based on the new appointment which brought about many different challenges related to International Business collaborations.

The main reason to highlight my career is to highlight the background that I have so that when I state facts about the 'Working Life', readers will know where I am coming from. I started as an Engineer in a technical role, aspired to be a manager and a leader. I did gain knowledge through experience and was fortunate to have so much of exposure in a Global environment.

BP FORTIES ALPHA

ON SITE MEXICO

BP FORTIES C PLATFORM

SITE IN ARGENTINA

BP FORTIES D PLATFORM

VIEW FROM HELICOPTER BP FORTIES OFFSHORE FIELD

HANNOVER SHOW WELCOMING DUKE OF GLOUSCESTER

# AROUND THE WORLD IN…….… 65 YEARS

"To move, to breathe, to fly, to float; to gain all while you give; to roam the roads of lands remote; to travel is to live." — Hans Christian Andersen

This book is all about sharing experiences so that people can benefit from information imparted. There are millions of books and active social media sites which give you wonderful insights into visiting some of the greatest places on earth. Thus, it is with a humble bow, I offer my own choice of places that are different and unusual to be considered for a visit should the opportunity arise. The places mentioned in this chapter have not been covered elsewhere in the book.

PARIS – This has to be the most romantic city on the earth. A dinner on the Bateaux Mouche cruising on the river Seine is best described by someone as,

"The sun sets and night falls over Paris, the flagship Jean-Sébastien Mouche casts off its moorings and the harbour slowly drifts away. You are about to experience an extraordinary dinner cruise with the company Bateaux Mouches® … The violin and the piano begin to play in tune and the city of lights slowly unveils itself as you softly slip by along the shimmering waters of the Seine. The mood is romantic, the magic is in force…You are the actors in a wonderful play, played only for you. The sophisticated menu echos the extraordinary setting, displaying culinary flair, governed by excellence. This dinner cruise will be remembered as one of the most special moments of your stay in Paris."

There are other extraordinary experiences:

- An evening walk on the Elegant Champs D' Elysees from near Arc de Triomphe to the Plaza Concorde

- Another dinner on the Le Jules Verne on the second floor of the Eiffel Tower, a rare culinary as well as a romantic experience.

- Have to catch one of the famous Paris shows at Moulin Rouge. Although Lido and Crazy Horse offer equally good shows as well.

- Montmartre perched high on the 'Butte' (Paris's highest and most northerly hill), the area is tightly packed with houses, spiralling round the mound below the sugary-white dome of the Sacré-Coeur. Despite the thronging tourists (chiefly around Place du Tertre) it remains the most unabashedly romantic part of Paris – a place in which to climb quiet stairways, peer down narrow alleys onto ivy-clad houses, and watch the world go by in atmospheric cafés – especially along Rue des Abbesses, Rue des Trois Frères and Rue des Martyrs. Artists have historically been attracted to Montmartre since Renoir and Toulouse-Lautrec immortalised the cabarets here in the late 19th century; even today an arty vibe lives on thanks to the upwardly-mobile film, music and media types that have moved in.

CHICAGO -A city of neighbour hoods, Chicago is wholly unique and no matter where you go, each part has its own draw: the buzzing Loop downtown and upscale River North, artsy Wicker Park, scholarly Hyde Park, and flamboyant Boys town. Add to that some of the world's best architecture and museums, a thriving music and dining scene, and its multi-cultural make-up, and you'll see why for many, the Second City is second to none. Each neighbourhood offers its own unique features including the food offerings. Walking through some of the Italian areas you suddenly feel that you are walking in the footsteps of Al Capone!

Whether you're in the mood for comedy, jazz clubs, fine dining, glittering skyscrapers, or an afternoon of shopping, T+L's Chicago travel guide has the scoop on where to go. During the 19th century, Chicago was a major hub for the shipping industry; present day Chicago is better known for its vibrant music scene—the city played a seminal role in the emergence of jazz and blues, and its symphony orchestra is a standout—but its history as a major port city is still reflected in Chicago's vibrant waterfront district.


It's best to visit Chicago in the spring or in fall, when temperatures are warm and the city offers plenty of festivals and activities. Peak travel season occurs during the summer months, when the weather is at its warmest—though the high season means larger crowds and higher prices at hotels. Winters in Chicago can be chilly and snowy, but you may want to brave a blizzard or two for the lower airfare and hotel prices. When you arrive, the Midwestern friendliness will stay with you no matter what's happening outside.

SAN FRANCISCO

A fascinating city which has been the setting for many Hollywood classical movies.  With the rolling mist and the steep rolling hills and the imposing site of the Golden Gate Bridge it is a unique setting. There is also the grand Oakland bay Bridge but not as famous as the other one. There are over fifty hills in the city and one of the most popular way to get up and down are the legendary cable cars of this city. Very popular with the tourists, there is nothing more prestigious then to hang on the cable car's steps especially on the downhill journeys. The Water front is the place of restaurants at Fisherman's Wharf and the increasingly popular Pier 39

The eclectic architecture gives the city a special character and no wonder it is so popular with the Hollywood fraternity. Due to its geographical location on some unstable earth plates, the place is always likely to experience tremors but that does not dim the interest of millions of tourists.

The city is famed for liberalizing attitudes, along with the rise of the "hippie" counterculture, the Sexual Revolution, the Peace Movement growing from opposition to United States involvement in the Vietnam War, and other factors led to the Summer of Love and the gay rights movement, cementing San Francisco as a centre of liberal activism in the United States.

Sailing onto the bay, the ever changeable weather can dictate the type of tour one might have. Regardless one cannot miss the Alcatraz this was the site of the first lighthouse in the Western United States but became a federal penitentiary from 1934-1963, housing famous convicts such as Al Capone and George "Machine Gun" Kelly. Now, this once infamous prison island is part of the Bay Area's 80,000-acre Golden Gate National Recreation Area. A tour of the site is a little bit 'uneasy' as one can witness the prison blocks and the small confinement areas. Subject of many movies but I was pleased to get off this island perhaps due to the claustrophobia.

In and around San Francisco are quaint areas e.g. a ferry ride away the tour of Sausalito or a drive through the NAPA valley where the finest Californian wines are produced.

For me the city holds great romantic memories. At about the time I met the love of my life, Annie, as we were in the early stages of discovering each other. We attended the George Washington Ball organized annually by the American expatriate community in Kuala Lumpur. As fate would have it

I won the grand raffle prize which was holiday for two to Tokyo and San Francisco with complimentary stays at the Hilton in both cities and free return travel by United Airlines. Thus we had our honeymoon before getting married perhaps not a bad concept at that.


LOS ANGELES

LA as popularly known is one of the largest cities in the USA and parts of it are very thickly populated. My main purpose was to visit Hollywood and take a walk on Rodeo drive. Both of these two things I did in style but was not prepared by so much more that this city has to offer. The down town is very impressive and I had not realized the large sized mountains that surround LA and add to the character of the place. I must admit I got hooked to the Bay area and spent a lot of time exploring many of the beaches and just loosing myself for days in the ambience and the sights.

The city is truly multicultural with an historical and significant Hispanic and Latino presence, African Americans and the latter immigration bringing in the Asians. LA has one of the largest China towns. The main reason of pointing out the cultural diversity is the fusion of social life and food.


RIO DE JANIERO

This is a pure fun city and just to visit is a great experience but to have the opportunity to visit during the Carnival week is just good fortune. The first time in Rio was a few hours in transit but the whole place was buzzing as it was the Carnival week. Just thinking about it I was tempted to miss the connecting flight but somehow the sense of duty prevailed and I missed the opportunity. I returned a few weeks later but the Carnival was over. Nevertheless I always had the ambition to stand next to Christ the Redeemer statue on the Corvocado   having seen it in many movies. I took a trip to the Sugar Loaf mountains and relaxed mostly on the Ipanema beach as the hotel had a part of it as their private domain. This at the time was a major consideration in terms of safety as muggings were rife day and night in the open. One of the reasons I did not spend too much time on the famous Copacabana beach was just that problem.

Having done the sites, the true magic of Rio is the night and the Samba!!! I be-friended a bar man in the hotel who introduced me to Caiprihania. He was a typical warm hearted Brazilian and told me where the best places were located to catch the Samba performances. He talked a lot about the Carnival and convinced me to return one day and he promised to help and keep me safe. He organized his taxi driver friends to take me out at night in search of Samba bars and also to remain by my side to protect me. Within the Lapa area there were some wonderful places to listen to the music. However, it was when I was taken to some places deep inside the city that the local scene emerged and I entered bars which I would never have ventured into on my own. People were always friendly and always partying and swaying to the rhythms of the Samba. Brazilians never tire of partying or listening and dancing to the Samba and the way they move an gyrate is magic in itself.

I kept in touch with my friend Salazar and returned two years later at the time of Carnival. I booked the hotel early and paid about five times the previous rate for 4 nights. Salazar had made all the arrangements for me to get a ticket to one of the better arenas in the Sambadrome to be able to see the Wonderful and the symbolic parade. Like many Brazilians he had turned a Carnival guide for that season and the best thing was he had a group of Americans whom I joined to maintain safety in numbers. The days before the Carnival we followed our guide. This was partying like never before or ever since then. Parties went on all night in cafes, clubs, streets with music and plentiful supply of drinks. One had to be careful where the drinks were coming from but we always had our guardian. It was good to be in a group to be a little bit safe and belong but the temptations were there in form of beautiful scantily clad ladies. One had to be careful as there was an equal number of transvestites! Of course one cannot go in too much detail.

The finale was the Carnival parade and what can one say, some of the floats and displays are beyond imagination and the amount of work that must go into making these has to be admired. The Carnival reflects every aspect of Brazilian life, culture and their history and in some ways it is their identity for the rest of the world.

ARGENTINA – BUONES AIRES - THE TRIPLE FRONTIER    - IGUAZU FALLS - BARILOCHE – LOS GLACIARES

Arriving in Buenos Aires was a surprise as it seemed just like a European city and not the capital of a Latin American nation. The infra-structure the wide avenues, the boulevards and the architecture of the buildings definitely highlights the Spanish influence. It is one of the most prosperous cities in South America and the local people go out of their way to emphasize the point. Another amusing fact is that most Argentinians always claim to be the direct descendants of pure Spanish blood and state that they are not really Latin Americans. One thing is for certain, the Argentinians have a rich heritage in the Arts, Culture & music.  The Rio de Plata is known as the Capital of Tango and the display by professional dancers are breath taking in this art form.

Of course Argentinian Grass fed beef is well known all over the world and apart from some very great restaurants all over the country. If one could get invited to a local Asado de Parilla then the meaning of Barbeque will change for them forever. The local wines or of very good quality and lately becoming popular around the world.

The city has a great history but among the most recent is the legend of Eva Peron and the memories of the so called dirty war on left wing dissidents. In the latter Government was responsible for the disappearance of thousands of young men attributed to the control of Communism. Latin America did face the rise of Leftist influence in the 50s, 60s and 70s and also the famous revolutionary Che Guehvera was an Argentinian and in some quarters a real hero.

Another tradition in Argentina is to have a communal drinking session with Mate. Mate is a traditional drink in some countries neighbouring Argentina. The drink, which contains mateine (an analog of caffeine), is made by an infusion of dried leaves of yerba mate. It is usually drunk with friends and served in a hollow calabash gourd with a "Bombilla", a special metallic drinking straw. It is traditionally made of silver. Like other brewed herbs, yerba mate leaves are dried, chopped, and ground into a powder called yerba. The bombilla is both a straw and a sieve. The end which is placed in the drink is wider, with small holes or slots that let the brewed liquid in, but block the chunky matter that makes up much of the mixture. After the brew the Gourd is passed around for a few sips and so forth

The Triple Frontier (Spanish: La Triple Frontera, Portuguese: Tríplice Fronteira) is a tri-border area along the junction of Paraguay, Argentina, and Brazil, where the Iguazú and Paraná rivers converge. Near the convergence are the cities of Ciudad del Este, Alto Paraná; Puerto Iguazú, Misiones and Foz do Iguaçu, Paraná. This area is near Iguazú Falls and the Itaipú hydroelectric plant. The Triple Frontier is an important tourist area, within the touristic sub region of the Región de las Aguas Grandes. Visitors can see the Tancredo Neves Bridge, which connects the Argentine city of Puerto Iguazú and its Brazilian neighbor, Foz do Iguaçu. At the convergence of the borders, each of the three bordering countries has erected an obelisk, painted in the national colours of the country in which it is located. All three countries can be seen from each of the obelisks. There are only a few other places in the world which have such a unique geographical location.

Not far from the triple frontier are the Iguazu falls perhaps not so well known outside this continent. Situated in Iguazú National Park, some 20 km. from Puerto Iguazú in the north of the province of Misiones, Argentina, the Iguazú falls are shared with Brazil. There are over 200 falls and this is an area of great natural beauty.

Bariloche is perhaps the largest Ski Resort in the Southern Hemisphere. As you can imagine a lot of tourists head for this beautiful area with many lakes, ski slopes and sights similar to Switzerland. I was fortunate that work took me to this resort to Commission a Gas turbine generator to add to the power capacity of this area.

The name of this city has some mysterious claims of links with Nazis who escaped Germany after the Second World War. During my visit I was disturbed by the presence of a German School in this city and many German styled Beer bars. Of course in the Northern part of Argentina which was an acknowledged refuge for many Nazis after the Second World War the German culture was more visible.

I quote,

'In 1995, Bariloche made headlines in the international press when it became known as a past haven for Nazi war criminals, such as the former SS Hauptsturmführer Erich Priebke. Priebke had been the director of the German School of Bariloche for many years.

In his 2004 book Bariloche nazi-guía turística, Argentine author Abel Basti claims that Adolf Hitler and Eva Braun lived in the surroundings of Bariloche for many years after the Second World War. Basti said that the Argentine Nazis chose the estate of Inalco as Hitler's refuge.

Grey Wolf: The Escape of Adolf Hitler, a 2011 book (and subsequent film) by British authors Simon Dunstan and Gerrard Williams, proposed that Hitler and Eva Braun escaped from Berlin in 1945 and hid at Hacienda San Ramon, six miles east of Bariloche, until the early 1960s. These accounts are disputed by most historians, who generally believe that Hitler and Braun committed suicide in the last days of the Second World War. During the dictatorship period many members of this community relocated to German colonies in Southern Chile under the protection of Chilean Dictator Augusto Pinochet.'

Unquote

I must say from my own observations there was definitely presence of Germans in Bariloche and the north of the country and it must have included the Nazis who escaped with their fortune to Argentina and Chile towards the end of the World War II. However, the tales of Hitler and Eva Bruan defying the might of the allies to escape and live in Argentina will remain as good material for fictional literature.

In my quest to reach the seventh Continent of the world i.e. Antartica , I fell short by a long distance and only made it so far as the Los Galciaras national park. A rare place on earth. The park is famous for its massive ice cap, which is the biggest in the world outside of Antarctica and Greenland, and named after the multiple glaciers that form at its end. There are 47 large glaciers in Los Glaciares. Glaciers - masses of ice that slowly moves under its own weight - are what the national park is known for, and create its most visually stunning areas.

The glaciers in the park are unusual because they start at less than 1,500 metres above sea level compared to 2,500 metres for most glaciers, creating stunning views on the edge of its lakes.

CARIBBEAN – JAMAICA, BARBADOS, TRINIDAD &TOBAGO, ANITGUA

There is a magic and charm about travelling around the Caribbean islands blessed by great weather and the magnificent stretches of beautiful beaches and the wonderful sea. There are over 700 islands and most of these have unique beauty and charm. The Caribbean offers the rhythm the music, nonstop groovy parties and their own style of Cajun food amongst other spicy offerings. Of course the abundance of Rum has led to wonderful Cocktails being created and they just add to the relaxation aspect of any holiday in this part of the world.

Pick the timing of the visit is a must as there are periods when the region is hit by devastating Hurricanes with clockwork regularity.

 I pick only four islands to comment on although the first two have had turbulent times in the past making these somewhat a worrisome destination. By and large if visitors follow certain simple rules there would be no problems.

Jamaica – Many wonderful beaches on the island. The two large centres are Kingston and Ocho Rios. The latter was the setting of some of the scenes shot for the first James Bond Movie – Dr. No

Barbados - Adventure, romance, history and sport all come together in Barbados, a Caribbean island rich in travel experiences. Extraordinary sights and sounds await your visit, brushed with tropical breezes, filtered through year-round sunshine, and accompanied by star-studded nights. Each place has a story, each meal is a celebration, each day brings new discoveries that you will remember forever. Many of our visitors find that a once-in-a-lifetime experience turns into a treasured repeat performance. Barbados makes the best holiday experiences year after year after year. ...... (Anon)

Trinidad and Tobago – An island very close to the South American mainland and a little different to the other islands. The population is influenced by the Latin American culture. Many of the European settlers came and set up home here as well. The British brought in many nationalities after the emancipation of slavery. People from China, India and Portugal. Currently, the Indian Community has a sizeable population on the island.

The amalgamation of different cultures and the beautiful geographical layout featuring beautiful beaches makes it a popular destination.

Anitgua – A smaller island towards East Caribbean. It has perhaps the most beautiful beaches in the whole of Caribbean. There are many remnants of the British Colonial rule.

EGYPT – PYRAMIDS

The concept of the burial of powerful kings in massive chambers with wealth and other offerings is a fascinating concept as structure similar to Pyramids exist in Egypt, South and Central America and China .Apart from the great distances involved the relevant time periods have massive gaps. The customs and patterns of the burials are alarmingly similar.

Nevertheless the three great Pyramids Khufu, Khafre, and Menkaure— correspond to the kings for whom these were built and the Great Sphinx are erected on a rocky plateau on the West bank of the Nile near Giza area of Egypt. These were all built around 2550 -2490 B.C

These are awesome structures and a visit once in a lifetime is highly recommended.

ATHENS – ACROPOLIS

People visit Greece for all the beautiful Mediterranean Islands and the laid back style of life. Indeed there are some great islands and it would take another book to narrate the experiences in all the wonderful places. However, visiting the Acropolis in Athens which of course is a historical monument. It embodies all the myths and the history of the Greek Culture. It is a special feeling being there and perhaps it is the elevated location that makes it so.

SWITZERLAND – ST.MORITZ – MT.TITLIS – JUNGFRAU – ZAMERATT

One of the most 'comfortable' countries to visit with its clean air and efficient services. The country has the iconic landmark the Alps that surround the nine so called Alpine countries.

ST.MORITZ

I always had fascination to visit St.Moritz because it was always mentioned in songs, fiction and no. fiction books as a place being the playground of the rich and famous.  It is a high Alpine resort in the Engadine in Switzerland, at an elevation of about 1,800 metres (5,910 ft) above sea level. It is Upper Engadine's major village and a municipality in the district of Maloja in the Swiss canton of Graubünden. The city's view is dominated by the Lej da San Murezzan or Lake of St.Moritz.


## MOUNT TITILIS

At 10,000 feet, Mount Titlis, is Central Switzerland's loftiest peak exuding a snow and ice spectacular that's visually stunning. And, this journey in Switzerland is even more camera-compulsory because you'll be riding in the revolving Rotair, an aerial cable car that delivers awesome 360-degree panoramic views of the snow-covered valleys, glaciers, lakes, forests, and mountains in Switzerland. As anywhere else in Switzerland this peak is very popular with the Indian tourists who are inspired to visit as large number of Bollywood movies take advantage filming in the beautiful locations around this country.

## JUNGFRAU

For more than 100 years, the Jungfrau railway has been making its journey to Europe's highest-altitude railway station at 3454 metres a.s.l. — right at the heart of the UNESCO heritage site "Swiss Alps Jungfrau-Aletsch". All through the year, the cog railway runs steeply up through a tunnel to the Jungfraujoch from Kleine Scheidegg.

The tunnel leading up from the station Eigergletscher is seven kilometres in length and was built between 1896 and 1912. One stop within the tunnel offers spectacular views onto the glacier world outside through windows in the Eiger North Face. On the summit, visitors are greeted by a high-Alpine wonder world made of ice, snow and rocks. All of this can be marvelled at from the viewing platforms "Sphinx" and "Plateau" on the Aletsch glacier or from the "Ice Palace".

The Jungfrau peak was used as a location in the James Bond movie "On Her Majesty's Secret Service ".

## ZERMATT

Zermatt is a car-free village in the upper Valais, one of the alpine cantons of Switzerland. It's probably best known as a platform for skiing and mountaineering, especially on the mountain which towers above the village, the mystical Matterhorn. The other famous ride is Gornergrat Railway, a ride to the top of Mount Gornergrat.

One of the best ways around Switzerland is to use the highly efficient train service to see the wonderful sites. The train company is linked into the other tourist institutions and hence it just makes it that much more convenient to have a Period Rail ticket. One of the most outstanding trips by rail in Switzerland is the ride on the Glacier Express from Zemratt to St.Moritz

## ITALY – ROME – VENICE – FIRENZE

Italy has left a major impact on Western culture and food. It has the great and unparalleled history and legacy in arts & culture. Its geographical layout gives it lakes, mountains and special regions e.g. the paradise like Tuscany region. Being a peninsula the country has an extended coast line and some unique islands surrounded by the Mediterranean. The sovereign states of San Marino and the Vatican City are enclaves within Italy, while Campione d'Italia is an Italian exclave in Switzerland.

Vatican City of course is a great centre of the Catholic religion and houses the official residence of the Pope.    Within Vatican City are religious and cultural sites such as St. Peter's Basilica, the Sistine Chapel and the Vatican Museums. They feature some of the world's most famous paintings and sculptures. The unique economy of Vatican City is supported financially by the sale of postage stamps and tourist mementos, fees for admission to museums, and the sale of publications.

## ROME

Rome is one of the greatest cities of the world built on seven hills and with a legendary tale of having been founded by Romulus and Remus the twin brothers who were brought up by a 'she-wolf '. The city has many famous tourist landmarks such as the Colloseum, The Trevi Fountain, The Altarre della Patria, Pallatine Hill etc

## FIRENZE

Florence, (Firenze) capital of Italy's Tuscany region, is home to many masterpieces of Renaissance art and architecture. One of its most iconic sights is the Duomo, a cathedral with a terracotta-tiled dome engineered by Brunelleschi and a bell tower by Giotto. The Galleria dell'Accademia displays Michelangelo's "David" sculpture. The Uffizi Gallery exhibits Botticelli's "The

Birth of Venus" and da Vinci's "Annunciation. The surrounding Tuscany region is paradise on earth with temperate climate and the best Chianti wines.


VENICE

Venice is a unique city and whatever one hears about it means nothing until you get there and experience the magic and splendour of the place. It is a city built on canals connecting 118 islands. No words could do justice to this place but a ride on the famous Gondola soon puts one in a surreal state.


RUSSIA

I visited the Soviet Union just before the break up and was able to experience a diluted 'cold war' ambience but there was no longer the mystique associated with a KGB dominated environment. Watching too many movies on the cold war had created an intrigue about how life was really like in a strict Communist state where one was 'always being watched.' What I experienced was a sad state of affairs and a great nation on its knees. Sure at the airport KGB personnel checked Passports but these were smart ever so young looking men instead of the tough and scar faces that one saw in the movies of that time. The hotels were all State controlled and upon check in one had to slip ten dollar bills to be assured of a better room. The Passport had to be surrendered for a check by KGB. On each floor there was a large sized female who controlled the key movements and also handed over the daily ration of toilet paper which was three strips of the roughest paper ever. Other than that if you had on you US$ Dollars you could enjoy the best of Moscow's diners, bars and night clubs. It was not a good feeling when one saw long queues outside food stores and supermarkets and unhealthy strips of fat being sold and the foreigners went into affluent restaurants to have the best of the Russian cuisine with the finest Vodka and Brandies.

Moscow is unique with the Kremlin, the Red square and the St.Basil's cathedral as stand out landmarks. Although the Stalin's mausoleum in the red square where his embalmed body lies in eternal rest is not my favourite site of Moscow. There are other similar sites for Lenin in Leningrad, Mao in Tiananmen Square and I believe for Mr.Kim in Pyongyang. This kind of morbid human worship is a part of the Communist doctrine but to me is a disrespect of the dead.

Some of the most impressive sites in Moscow are the Metro stations especially the one's closer to the city centre. These are magnificent buildings and structures of great period architecture and with heavy use of marble.  There is no comparison with other urban transport systems anywhere in the world. The metro trains were at that time very clean and the service was very good. The cost was a few coins which frankly had no value but was a symbolic gesture to pay for the service.

After a few days of visiting many great museums including inside the Kremlin and enjoying some of the finest restaurants of the time, I flew to Minsk. Domestic travel at that time was no better than the one in China at the same time period. Minsk is now the capital of Belarus but at that time was a state capital. Going deeper in the country more depravation became visible. It was that time when the Russian people had started to realize that for 70 years they had been oppressed and led on a false path which led to nowhere. The older generation were at that time accepting their fate and looked defeated in life. This was very sad to see as most of these people were very nice human beings and very competent and capable in their own field of speciality. In spite of the prolonged sanctions the Soviet Engineers and technicians had found a way around most innovative challenges.

One night while still in Minsk, I was woken by a phone call with a very soft female voice making a statement of which I could not understand a single word. I Thought it was the lady of the night who was trying to probably tell me that the 'LADY GUARDIANS '  watching over all the rooms on our floor had gone to sleep and …. ? I kept saying, "No, Thank you." repeatedly but not to much avail. After a few calls she stopped and said Paseba which meant thank you and said something else and put the phone down. Of course I was totally disturbed and was expecting a knock on the door or someone breaking the door down and dragging me out. First thing that I did was to put some shorts on as I always sleep in my birth attire. After a very sleepless night, I was keen to get the help of our Russian host and he seemed to be definitely KGB as he flashed his ID card to the reception and enquired quite rudely as to why his guest was disturbed at night.It turned out the that Security bureau (KGB) had finally got around to checking my Passport and apparently the Russian Embassy in London had not endorsed for me to be able to enter Minsk as only my final destination Orsha within the state of Belarus was mentioned. Thus, I had broken the local law and needed to leave Minsk by noon that day. We were set to leave for Orsha so further tension was avoided. Months later I returned to Minsk with a proper endorsement and had a very good stay and in fact took a train from there to Warsaw which was another adventure.

Driving through the country side revealed the depravation of the rural people and it just did not seem like being in the second most powerful nation of the world but some third world state.

We arrived at a massive Machine tool manufacturing complex near Orsha which was a city in itself. This was a by-product of the Stalin era. A self-sufficient Manufacturing complex which housed over 3000 employees and their families. All the social and cultural facilities were on site e.g. Schools, Sport clubs, hospitals, social halls etc. The Company management even arranged marriages amongst its workers. To sustain it they manufactured large Machine tools for the rest of the Soviet Industry and the Defence forces. Their ready made export markets were the other satellite Soviet bloc nations, China, India, Libya, to a small extent Cuba and some of the other African nations under their influence. Since the Glasnots the Soviet bloc countries had started to break away and the units such as these suffered from severe downturn in their regular business and were desperately seeking investments and new markets to sustain themselves and their way of life.

Needless to say we were accorded the most warm welcome and provided the best accommodation at their VIP guest house. We were taken to the massive Sauna baths and pinned against the walls and given a beating with shrubs a la Scandinavian style. The only disappointment were the toilet facilities which were simply holes in the ground and a pole to hold on to. For the first time I was pleased to have a large frame as I was much bigger than the hole and was not just going to slip down in case the hand slipped.

Back to Moscow and the Bolshoi ballet. Some strings had to be pulled to get us in. The performance was Rodin but it could have been anything. Just being there was like a dream. There is no doubt that in terms of Arts and culture and ballet the Russians are the best.

DUBAI

A city and a Emirate the largest part of the United Arab Emirates. Its precipitous rise to a Luxury centre from a simple Shipping and a trading centre is one of the modern day miracles.

Its skyline is impressive and without parallel anywhere in the world. Structures like the Burj Al Khalifa the tallest building in the world and Burj Al Arab the most luxurious hotel in the world and the opulent surroundings are surreal and for ordinary people hard to grasp.

Since it is meant to be a luxury resort it is a centre for nightlife, food, night and desert safaris, theme and amusement parks backed up by some of the finest hotels in the world. Nothing is cheap in this city but well worth a visit if one wants a different type of escape from reality. It is all created and nothing is natural except the desert but so much thought has gone into appealing to the human senses that it has become one of the major entertainment centres of the world.

MAKKAH - MEDINA

Like every Muslim, I have found my visits to the two holy cities spiritually stimulating and enlightening.


INDIA

India is truly one of the greatest countries of the world with one of the oldest civilizations. Rich in ancient traditions and culture it is a unique nation of many different sub –cultures, religions and beliefs. As an estimate some hundreds of dialects are spoken around the country. Although there are only two official national languages i.e. Hindi and English and over twenty state and regional official languages

India is the seventh largest country in area and the second largest in terms of population. The geographical terrain varies from the highest peaks of the world in the Himalayas to the plains and deserts in the centre and more tropical regions down south. Undoubtedly, a fascinating place to visit and it would take many visits just to get a grasp of what is on offer.

Modern India has risen to be one of the great powers of the world in every sense of the word. India is poised to take place among the top nations of the world and be a part of the elite.

As mentioned before, there is so much to do and see that it is difficult to highlight the best. I can go by my experience and point out some of the easier places to get to. Any aspiring visitor to India must go there with an open heart and not expect everything to be perfect. With the right attitude a visit to India can be the greatest experience in life as there really are so many different things to see, so many wonderful dishes to be tasted and so much warm and genuine hospitality to be enjoyed.


NEW DELHI

Delhi is the capital of India and by any standards a large city with a population of around 22m people. Some areas are truly congested but that is not a surprise. The contrasts are amazing, as this city retains its monuments and vestiges from the time of the Mughal dynasties of four hundred years ago to the British colonial layouts and buildings. In relative terms, Delhi is less of a chaos as it has a defined structure and with the addition of a MRT service it has become easier to get around.

Wonderful ancient monuments e.g. Qutab Minar, the Red fort, Mughal Emperor Humayan's tomb, the Jamia Masjid (Mosque) are very interesting places to visit. The latter monuments and buildings reflect the colonial past and the present strengths e.g. The India gate, the Rajpath, The President's palace and the Lok Sabah (Parliament).

All the top hotel brands are in New Delhi and provide comfortable accommodation and the traditional Indian hospitality.The Centre of the City i.e. the Connaught square is the best place to shop for tourists

To really get to know this city, a visit to the Old Delhi is a must and that may be a bit cumbersome but it is worth it to understand how the majority of the locals live. Some of the traditional North Indian food available in old Delhi is the best in the world e.g. Butter Naan and Chicken Tikka and various type of Dhall.

AGRA

From New Delhi a train ride of about two hours takes you to Agra with world famed and the glorious Taj Mahal. It stands out in its total splendour and is most definitely a true Wonder of the world. Of and on it was the Capital of the Mughal Empire and was then known as Akbarabad named after the great Emperor, Akbar.

The Taj Mahal was built by the Emperor Shah Jahan to immortalize his love for one of his wives, the Empress Nur Jahan.

There are many other World Heritage sites in and around Agra such as:

Agra Fort

Agra Fort (sometimes called the Red Fort), was commissioned by the conquering Mughal Emperor Akbar the Great in 1565, and is another of Agra's World Heritage Sites.

The fort is crescent shaped, flattened on the east with a long, nearly straight wall facing the river. It has a total perimeter of 2.4 kilometres (1.5 mi), and is ringed by double castellated ramparts of red sandstone punctuated at regular intervals by bastions.

The fort is a typical example of Mughal architecture, effectively showing how the North Indian style of fort construction differed from that of the South.

Fatehpur Sikri

Dīwān-i-Khās – Hall of Private Audience

The Mughal Emperor Akbar built Fatehpūr Sikrī about 35 km (22 mi) from Agra, and moved his capital there.

Buland Darwāza or 'the lofty gateway' was built by the great Mughal emperor, Akbar in 1601 CE. At Fatehpūr Sikrī. Black and white marble inlays. An inscription on the central face of the Buland Darwāza demonstrates Akbar's religious broadmindedness, it is a message from Jesus advising his followers not to consider this world as their permanent home.

I'timād-Ud-Daulah[edit]

The Itmad-Ud-Daulah's Tomb at Agra

The Empress Nūr Jahān built I'timād-Ud-Daulah's Tomb, sometimes called the "Baby Tāj", for her father, Mirzā Ghiyās Beg, the Chief Minister of the Emperor Jahāngīr. a jewel box. Its garden layout and use of white marble, pietra dura, inlay designs and latticework presage many elements of the Tāj Mahal.

Tomb of Akbar the Great

Sikandra, the last resting place of the Mughal Emperor Akbar the Great, is on the Delhi-Agra Highway, only 13 kilometres (8.1 miles) from the Agra Fort. Akbar's tomb reflects the completeness of his personality. The vast, beautifully carved, red-ochre sandstone tomb with deers, rabbits and langurs is set amidst a lush garden. Akbar himself planned his own tomb and selected a suitable site for it. To construct a tomb in one's lifetime was a Turkic custom which the Mughals followed religiously.

Jamā Masjid [edit]

The Jāma Masjid is a large mosque attributed to Shah Jahan's daughter, Princess Jahanara Begum, built in 1648, notable for its unusual dome and absence of minarets.

Chīnī kā Rauza

Notable for its Persian influenced dome of blue glazed tiles, the Chīnī kā Rauza is dedicated to the Prime Minister of Shāh Jahān, 'Allāma Afzal Khāl Mullā Shukrullāh of Shiraz.

Rām Bāgh

The oldest Mughal garden in India, the Rām Bāgh was built by the Emperor Bābar in 1528 on the bank of the Yamuna. It lies about 2.34 km (1 mi) north of the Tāj Mahal. The pavilions in this garden are designed so that the wind from the Yamuna, combined with the greenery, keeps them cool even during the peak of summer.

Mariam's TombMariams Tomb, is the tomb of Mariam, the wife of great Mughal Emperor Akbar. The tomb is within the compound of the Christian Missionary Society.

Mehtāb Bāgh

Plan of the Taj complex with the Mehtab Bagh gardens to the left

The Mehtāb Bāgh, or 'Moonlight Garden', is on the opposite bank of the River Yamuna from the Tāj Mahal.

Keetham Lake [edit]

Also known as Sur Sarovar, Keetham Lake is situated about 7 kilometres (4.3 miles) from the Akbar tomb in Agra, within the Surdas Reserved Forest. The lake has an impressive variety of aquatic life and water birds.

JAIPUR

Jaipur is the capital of India's Rajasthan state. It evokes the royal family that once ruled the region and that, in 1727, founded what is now called the Old City, or "Pink City" for its trademark building colour. At the center of its stately street grid (notable in India) stands the opulent, colonnaded City Palace complex. With gardens, courtyards and museums, part of it is still a royal residence. It hosts several attractions like the City Palace, Govind Dev ji Temple, Vidhan Sabha, Birla Temple, several massive Rajput forts and so on. It also serves as a stepping stone for travellers heading to the desert cities of Jodhpur and Jaisalme.

Many palaces, forts and gardens to visit. Like anywhere in India the local cuisine offers variety and scrumptious dishes.


THAILAND

As a child when I used to envisage the Far East as lands of paddy fields, Elephants, beautiful temples and palaces, people with straw hats etc etc

Thailand is that country and one of the greatest places in Asia to visit. It is a popular tourism place and the people and the Government of Thailand priortize tourism as one of their key economic sectors. As a result a lot of facilities and guidance is available for all visitors.

Thailand previously known as Siam has always had a bit of a sleazy image and thankfully it is now receding as other sleaze centres take shape elsewhere in the region. I am not going to dwell on this subject but most definitely one does see some very disturbing sites in Thailand related to the ugly flesh trade.

Thailand has gone through much political upheaval in the last ten years as it tries to grapple the spirit of democracy and this has cast some shadow over the tourism sector. Report of political rallies and disturbances are enough to put of budding tourists. Furthermore, since the passing away of their revered King Bhumibol Adulyadej (Rama IX). His son King Vajiralongkorn (or Rama X) may never get the same respect and standing as his father and remains to be seen if the monarchy will survive.

Bangkok, Thailand's capital, is a large city known for ornate shrines and vibrant street life. The boat-filled Chao Phraya River feeds its network of canals, flowing past the Rattanakosin royal district, home to opulent Grand Palace and its sacred Wat Phra Kaew Temple. Nearby is Wat Pho Temple with an enormous reclining Buddha and, on the opposite shore, Wat Arun Temple with its steep steps and Khmer-style spire. There are many historical sites to visit including the Grand Palace. There are many nearby places to visit for half or full day tours e.g. The Rose gardens, The Elephant Football game and the tour to the ancient Capital Ayutthaya. The latter tour can be done by taking the bus in the morning and visiting all the wonderful historical sites and then return by luxurious boat in the afternoon sailing on the Chao Priya river taking in the sights of the many people who live on houses built on the water. Coming into Bangkok you can see the impressive skyline with the modern buildings and catch site of great hotels like the Shangri La and the Mandarin Oriental. The latter is considered the finest hotel in Asia

Another major attraction near to Bangkok is the floating market, Damnoen Saduak continues to offer an authentic experience despite its increasingly touristy atmosphere. Imagine dozens of wooden row boats floating by, each laden to the brim with farm-fresh fruits, vegetables or flowers. Food vendors fill their vessels with cauldrons and charcoal grills, ready to whip up a bowl of 'boat noodle' or seafood skewers upon request. This is something special.

 Bangkok's rapid growth amidst little urban planning and regulation has resulted in a haphazard cityscape and inadequate infrastructure systems. Limited roads, despite an extensive expressway network, together with substantial private car usage, have led to chronic and crippling traffic congestion, which caused severe air pollution in the 1990s. The city has since turned to public transport in an attempt to solve this major problem. Five rapid transit lines are now in operation, with more systems under construction or planned by the national government and the Bangkok Metropolitan Administration.

One does not need to find the night life in Bangkok it will find you!!! There is something everyone no matter what your taste. I would just like to say that one of the most entertaining nights is the lady boy Calypso Cabaret show.

The cultural show and dinner at Silom Village is an introduction the exquisite traditional Thai dancing.

Wining and dining once again caters for every taste and the two specials places in my experience are the Sky Bar on top of the Le Bua State Tower. For dinner there is no better food than the Thai cuisine. Of all the experiences around the world, the Thai food has to be in the top three and lately its global popularity verifies this claim

The Seafood Market and Restaurant in Bangkok, with its famous slogan "If it swims we have it", is a well-known, long running and absolutely enormous restaurant on Sukhumvit Soi 24. With around 50 chefs in their kitchen, seating available for up to 1,500 guests and a fun 'choose your own produce' dining concept, this really is one unique dining experience.

The Seafood Market and Restaurant really is like no other place we've eaten at in Bangkok or anywhere else in the world for that matter. The sheer size of the place and the unique buy-before-you-eat style make this a particularly fun and memorable dining experience. The array of fresh local and imported produce also proves that you don't have to go all the way to the beach to find exotic fresh seafood. It's all available in Bangkok!

If there is a better dish than the curried Crab that they prepare and serve in minutes, I have yet to taste it.

The other places to recommend are the Phuket Island in the Andaman Sea, Krabi and the Phi Phi islands and of the most natural and relaxing spots is the koh Samuai Island.

Of course one cannot leave without enjoying the traditional Thai massage, a unique experience which definitely improves the blood circulation for days and relaxes the body beyond belief.

SINGAPORE

A small island state formed after political upheavals in the United Malay has become one of the most prosperous and opulent places to live in the world. After separating from the Federation of Malaysia the island state has prospered at the expense of being dominated by one political heirachy i.e. firstly by Mr.Lee Yuan Kew and then someone from outside the family and then his son. Everything works in Singapore but there are exasperating and somewhat draconian laws which cover every aspect of human behaviour. It is a great place to visit but only for a short time as most attractions can be covered in 4 days maximum. With one of the highest per capita income in the world, Singapore is like visiting Europe within Asia. There are some wonderful Colonial remnants like to the Raffles Hotel, worth a visit to enjoy the famous Singapore Cocktail. Its colonial core centers on the Padang, a cricket field since the 1830s and now flanked by grand buildings such as the City Hall, with its 18 Corinthian columns. In Singapore's Chinatown stands the red-and-gold Buddha Tooth Relic Temple, said to house one of Buddha's teeth. Amongst the modern attractions are the sky lift ride to the wonderful Sentosa Island which offers a variety of tourist activities. The fact that Singapore is a multi-cultural society even though it is dominated by the Chinese community, The Malays and Indians contribute to the diversity of the culture.  The Universal Studios complex and the casino are all set up to boost tourism. The fact that Singapore is a multi-cultural society even though it is dominated by the Chinese community, The Malays and Indians contribute to the diversity of the culture. and are one of the main reasons to visit Singapore.


INDONESIA – BALI

The mystical island of Bali is located within the Republic of Indonesia consisting of 17, 000 islands. In the midst of an area dominated by over 200 million Muslims this is a Hindu enclave.

Bali is an Indonesian island known for its forested volcanic mountains, iconic rice paddies, beaches and coral reefs. The island is home to religious sites such as cliff side Uluwatu Temple. To the south, the beachside city of Kuta has lively bars, while Seminyak, Sanur and Nusa Dua are popular resort towns. The island is also known for its yoga and meditation retreats.

The place has many romantic enclaves and the local culture adds to the mystical ambience.

The traditional Balinese dancing and the cultural shows which narrate ancient legendary stories in a drama act are highly original and a great experience.


AUSTRALIA – MELBOURNE – ADELAIDE – PERTH – SYDNEY – BRISBANE – PORT DOUGLAS – THE GREAT BARRIER REEF – ALURU

Australia is one of the most popular destination for people who live in and around Malaysia. For the people here this country is an alternative to travelling to Europe. Of course the two destinations could not be more contrasting.

Australia is a rugged country with a land mass that never seems to end. There is rare wild life not to be seen anywhere else e.g. Kangaroos, Koalas, Emus, Wallabies, etc

Australia has great beaches everywhere you go and many national Parks. In addition the centre of Australia is Uluru perhaps the centre of the Abroginial culture. This is surrounded by a massive desert with a peculiar reddish sand quite different to the deserts elsewhere in the world.

Then there is the World Heritage-listed Great Barrier Reef, which stretches for more than 2,000 kilometres along the Queensland coastline. This is the world's largest Coral reef. For snorkelling or Scuba diving the best in the world.

When the last century ended there was the talk of the Millenium bug which was supposed to bring the world to an end as the Computers ticked out. A group of my friends suggested we should get out of the way and go somewhere closer to the dateline and face the 'impending disaster' head on!! So we set up ahead of 31st Dec 1999 in Port Douglas and had one hell of a bash to welcome the new century. There was a cruise to the Great Barrier Reef and this is truly a fascinating place for the fact that it is unique.

For the British visitors, Australia is home form home in terms of most of the local traditions e.g. Pubs, Fish and chips etc. In spite of their Republican claims most of the Australians are loyal to the Queen. For a nation that was very cruel to its indigenous population and had an outright 'Whites only' immigration policy till about 40 years ago. They have made great strides in reforming the Social Charter and Australia is increasingly becoming a very multi-racial nation.

It is an affront to say so little about this great country but the few words have a strong sense.

For people who love sport this is the country which knows how to compete and mostly they are often the best in different disciplines of Sport. They also enjoy watch top level and competitive Sport. Being biased, I shall mention Cricket. Australians love their cricket and always strive to win and over the years they have had a sustained periods of being the top team. The Government of Australia supports the development of all national sports and invests a lot of money to create winners. There many famous Cricket grounds in Australia e.g. MCG in Melbourne, SCG in Sydney, The WACA in Perth and the GABBA in Brisbane. Arguably, the largest cricket ground in the world is the MCG and for the cricket lovers a visit to this place is a dream fulfilled.

The other sports that are worth watching live are the Australian Rules football derived from. Rugby and Gaelic football and Rugby Union. The true spirit of the Australian competitiveness truly comes out in top level games and can be spectacular to watch

## NEW ZEALAND – SOUTH ISLAND, NORTH ISLAND

Another part of the Commonwealth in the continent of Oceania. This must be the farthest distance from Great Britain yet the way of life and traditions are very British. Parts of the country look just like Scotland in a geographical sense.

New Zealand consists of two main islands and over six hundred smaller ones South and North Islands are the main land mass, both marked by volcanoes and glaciation. Both have great natural beauty in terms of mountains, lakes and other rare geographical layouts.

The South Island is the largest landmass of New Zealand and is the 12th largest island in the world. It is divided along its length by the Southern Alps .There are 18 peaks over 3,000 metres (9,800 ft), the highest of which is Aoraki / Mount Cook at 3,754 metres (12,316 ft). Fiordland's steep mountains and deep fiords record the extensive ice age glaciation of this south-western corner of the South Island. The North Island is the 14th largest island in the world and is less mountainous but is marked by volcanism.The highly active Taupo Volcanic Zone has formed a large volcanic plateau, punctuated by the North Island's highest mountain, Mount Ruapehu (9,177 ft). The plateau also hosts the country's largest lake, Lake Taupo.

New Zealand was home to many species of animals but very few have survived, while it still has very distinct creatures but unlike Australia these are more of a gentle type e.g. the Kiwi a bird without wings. Marine mammals however are abundant, with almost half the world's cetaceans (whales, dolphins, and porpoises) and large numbers of fur seals reported in New Zealand waters. Many seabirds breed in New Zealand, a third of them unique to the country. More penguin species are found in New Zealand than in any other country. Of course the New Zealanders fondly known as Kiwis always point out to their great tradition of farming and rearing lambs which outnumber the human population by a ratio of 4:1. Of course this brings in great economic benefits for the country.

The population mix is influenced by the proximity of the many South Sea Islands with many different races being an integral part of the society. Of course the indigenous people are the Maoris who have had a turbulent history but seem well integrated.

This is a highly developed country and it is a pleasure to visit and enjoy the great natural beauty and nothing is more exhilarating then to go on a whaling tour. Wonderful place to drive and see all the natural beauty spots. One of the best experiences if the season is right to go to enjoy a game of Rugby at the Eden Park, Auckland. Great ambience during big games and what was great to witness was the fact these occasions are also a family day out. It is pretty safe to take young children along and enjoy the event. This is very different to many other countries where going to sporting events can be an issue in terms of hooliganism and safety. This is an accolade to the character of the people of this nation who live by principles and uphold values which are rare elsewhere in the world.

HONORABLE MENTIONS

I may have missed out on some of the other great places to visit in a lifetime but will mention these as follows:

New York – The Big Apple; Barcelona; Scandanavia; Munich during the October Beer Fest; Istanbul; Mumbai;

THE WORST

At the risk of upsetting sentiments of the relevant nationals, I have to rec-count some of the worst experiences in visiting certain places. Perhaps the perception is based on my sole experience and perhaps I am being unfair. I offer my apologies if I am stepping on sensitivities.

LIBYA – TRIPOLI

I visited Tripoli in Dec1983 en route to an Oil & Gas installation in the Libyan Desert. To get the security pass to enter the Site in the desert one had to stop in Tripoli for a few days.

On the flight from Milan to Tripoli as I boarded the Libyan Airlines flight, my passport and everyone else's had to be inspected by burly air stewards, who were anything but what they were pretending to be. Some of the crew were European females who were not allowed to smile and most definitely did not engage in any type of conversation. During the flight we received the landing cards to fill in before arrival, these were all in Arabic so naturally I requested the air crew to help and they refused outright. I could not believe the situation upon looking around I noticed I was not the only one with this dilemma. There were smug looking frequent visitors sitting or dozing calmly. One such kind passenger handed me an English translation very discreetly when the burly crew were not looking.

Upon arrival at Tripoli airport the Customs and Immigration officials were as rude as they could be. After the release from all the mental stress, I was told that the Beach Hotel booked for me was not available after all, as the Late Col. Gaddafi and his entourage had commandeered the place for a few days. This meant the only other options were traditional hotels based on the 14th Century style! The one selected for me was in what could be best described as a slum area with open sewage. The hotel was like a tea house with lots of Libyans engaged in playing some form of cards and smoking all kinds of tobacco. The room was ancient, there were cob webs and in between was a 60 W bulb hanging from a cable. There was no visible mechanism to switch the light on or off. Later on I found out that the reception had the control and they switched off as they went to bed and switched on with their early shift. The bath room had a WC (thank God for little mercies), a mirror that had lost reflection properties a long time ago and a tap with reasonably cold and hot water control. Food was served in midst of the noisy crowd in the so called reception area which at best was a courtyard of an ancient house. Dinner was two choices Cold Cous Cous or cold Pasta (signs of Italian Colonialization). Breakfast was better as there was nice smelling fresh bread and strong Coffee. I was accompanied by another fellow Brit and that softened blows as he carried stocks of biscuits etc. Luckily, we were granted the Desert Pass very quickly and we were off.

The Desert Oil and Gas sites were run almost exclusively by the British expatriates and they ran these very professionally and the accommodation and facilities were reasonable. These guys were the best of best who worked hard but had a touch of the MASH crew about them i.e. making their own 'hooch' contravening strict local laws, having wild parties etc.


BRUNEI

One of the richest nations on earth as far as per capita income is concerned for the local people. However, there is not much to do. I am sure the locals have their own social escapes and I do believe the expatriates have developed their own clandestine sources of leisure.

ENJOYING RIO DE JANEIRO

# FABULOUS MEXICO

FABULOUS MEXICO

..... I dreamt of getting to Mexico from the age of about six, I made it at the age of 30.

.....The wait was worth it. It was everything I imagined it to be loud, colourful, chaotic, unruly but truly fabulous

..... There is something about Mexico which makes it the most exciting country in the world.

The Mexicans narrate an anecdote when asked to explain their country, "The Almighty must be a Mexican to allow so much chaos and yet people survive and a lot of them thrive."

When you cross the border from United States of America within a few meters is the United States of Mexico. Those few meters separate two contrasting worlds. I have often crossed one way or the other and suddenly stopped to contemplate this contrast but have never found any explanation.

In any case, I am very fond of Mexico and it is what it is. For me it is a very exciting place. I love its history, its culture, its music, its food and mostly the people. Apart from that it is geographically very varied with wonderful natural sites and some of the finest beaches in the world.

I could easily write a separate book on Mexico but instead I will just give a flavor based on my experiences in the country.

In the period that I lived in Mexico from 1981 to 1988 a lot happened in Mexico: serious economic crisis in 1982 and largely an unstable economic situation; Inflation often exceeding 80%; the Peso exchange rate to US$ deteriorating by a few hundred percent! ; The Chichonal volcano (not many know about it; the serious and tragic earthquakes in Mexico city in 1985, the Soccer World Cup 1986. Never did I ever see Mexicans give up hope and the fiestas came back even stronger after each untoward event.

I was based in the South East of the country in the State of Tabasco, the city of Villahermosa to be precise. There are four principal ecosystems in the state: tropical rainforest, tropical savannah, beaches and wetlands. Tropical rainforest dominates most of the state due to the high levels of rainfall the area receives. In short very hot and humid.

Here are a couple of narratives to highlight the character of the Mexican people.

In 1982, around April I woke up at my place of residence in Villahermosa and looked out of the window and I thought it was snowing!!! Suddenly it dawned on me that I was in the middle of a tropical city how could that be!!?? It had been a celebratory night before with much dancing and the Fiesta *spirits*. For a while I thought I had gone mad but decided to investigate further and dashed outside just about remembering to cover myself. Outside I found it was not snow but fine white dust. Something twigged in the brain about St.Helena volcano in the USA a few years earlier. That is what it was a Volcano some 50 kms away had erupted causing some serious devastation. I had to quickly acquaint myself with the precautions to be taken from the lovely looking fine dust as we had an expatriate staff of around 30 people who wanted assurances. Initially there was some panic as flights were cancelled and the roads became total jammed as people decided to run away from the area. There was a run on the Supermarkets and Food markets. The Government mobilized the Army and quickly brought the situation under control and calm prevailed. After the initial panic, I did not see any loss of Control and the Mexicans rose to help the victims in the affected areas. A different type of experience to live through in life!

The second incident was of a much larger magnitude and that was the devastating earthquakes that hit the heart of Mexico city in September 1985. I was not in The Capital at the time but got there 4 days later. It was impossible to believe how the land scape had changed in the Zona Rosa. Many buildings had collapsed and others were just simply squashed as if someone had swatted these with a heavy weight. It was the most disturbing experience to go around the City and talk to people. The death toll was heavy. There was a massive relief and rescue effort ongoing supported by the ordinary citizens of Mexico. Some were digging with their bare hands. There was no disorder or looting. Everyone was trying to locate survivors buried under the rabble. As an example our associate had an eighth floor office in a seventeen floor building which had just been swatted. Through sheer effort our associates with the help of volunteers dug through and brought out all the expensive belongings and some critical spare parts. I can only say that I was most touched by the spirit of the Mexicans in such a difficult hour. They rose to the occasion and made their nation proud of them.

As Mexico recovered from this great tragedy, concerns arose over the viability of the hosting of the 1986 Soccer World cup which was only eight months away at that time. Mexico had hosted a previous Soccer World Cup in 1970 which I had watched in awe on TV. Here arose a chance as Colombia the nominated hosts were going through some serious economic and political difficulties opted out and Mexico stepped in.

For Mexico to host the world cup of 1986 so soon after going through the tragedy of the earthquakes is a testimony to the nation. It was one of the most well organized Soccer events and I was fortunate to experience it firsthand. I attended most of the games held at the Aztec Stadium.That was an experience in itself at being in 120,000 seater stadium as opposed to The top clubs in the UK with some 30 – 35 K seats. It was not only the size but it was the ambience and the fiesta created by the Mexicans. This was the World Cup in which the famous 'Mexican Wave 'was created.


HISTORY AND CULTURE

In different part of the many states one can see the evidence of the ancient civilizations e.g. the main Olmec site in Tabasco is La Venta. 1400 - 400 B.C period of the Empire .The site covers an area of 5.3 square kilometres (2.0 sq mi) surrounded by swamps and marshes linked to the Tonalá River, 15 kilometres from the Gulf of Mexico. Around 300 AD, the Mayas began to dominate part of the state. Mayan sites include Comalcalco, Pomoná,  El Tortuguero and Jonuta. The Mayans in Tabasco reached their peak between the 6th and 7th centuries. In the neighbouring state of Chiapas are the more renowned remnants of Palenque to highlight the period of Mayan dominance. There are so many places to trace the fascinating Mesoamerican history. Travelling further South from Tabasco to Merida and to the Yucatan peninsula there are further sites. Chicen Itza quite close to Merida was one of the largest cities of the Mayans.

Teotihuacan is an ancient Mesoamerican city located in a sub-valley of the Valley of Mexico, located in the State of Mexico 40 kilometres (25 mi) northeast of modern-day Mexico City, known today as the site of many of the most architecturally significant Mesoamerican pyramids built in the pre-Columbian Americas. Often referred to as an Aztec civilization pyramids but there is a debate about this being the case. Apart from the pyramids, Teotihuacan is also anthropologically significant for its complex, multi-family residential compounds; the Avenue of the Dead; and the small portion of its vibrant murals that have been exceptionally well-preserved. Additionally, Teotihuacan exported fine obsidian tools that garnered high prestige and widespread usage throughout Mesoamerica.

I remember Mexico for such fascinating places and another book with many volumes could be written if one was to attempt to get to know most of the historical sites in Mexico.

Mexico City is one of the most exciting cities on the earth. At an altitude of 2240 metres and sitting on a lake and a soft base and facing endless possibilities of seismic activity.

The arts and culture as well as the music of Mexico is steeped in its history.

The ballet works and musical pieces reflect various regions and folk music genres of Mexico. Many of the ensemble's works reflect the traditions of indigenous Mesoamerican culture. Numbers of performers in individual dance numbers range from two to over thirty-five. There are three types of Ballet Folklorico: Danza, Mestizo, and Bailes Regionales (Regional dances).

The ensemble performs three times weekly at the Palace of Fine Arts in Mexico City. Sitting through the performances many times over, I was always totally enchanted because this a very special combination of local art and culture with traditional ballet. In my opinion this is one of the finest piece of art and culture anywhere in the world.

There are many traditional forms of art and dance and the country and it culture have abundant different forms. Some of the most popular and well known are the Mariachis and famous in dance tradition is the "Jarabe Tapatío", known as "Mexican hat dance". Traditional dancers perform a sequence of hopping steps, heel and toe tapping movements.

Nowhere reflects the soul of the Mexicans as well as the Plaza Gribaldi .The Plaza is known as Mexico City's home of mariachi music. At all hours of the day and night, mariachi bands can be found playing or soliciting gigs from visitors to the Plaza.The Salón Tenampa, which became the home of mariachi music in Mexico City in the 1920s, is still in business on the north side of the plaza. There is little point to go there in the early part of the night. The place livens up quite late and then remains vibrant till the early hours.

Few places in the world are as rich in museums as Mexico City.

Museo Nacional de Antropología: Occupying approximately 4,100 sq. m (44,132 sq. ft.), Mexico City's anthropology museum is regarded as one of the top museums in the world. It offers a mesmerizing, and encyclopedic, introduction to the culture of Mexico.

Museo Del Templo Mayor: Mexico City was once the capital of the vast Aztec empire, and on this very site, that civilization's most important temple stood. With style, and a good dollop of drama, the curators present the treasures that archaeologists dug up here—some 6,000-plus pieces.

Museo Casa de León Trotsky: Another house museum, but one with a gruesome backstory: Trotsky was killed here, after several attempts on his life. You'll see the bullet holes in the walls, though he was ultimately assassinated with an ice pick.

The Museo de Arte Moderno: This proud institution has the best permanent exhibition of painters and sculptors from the modern Mexican art movement, including important murals by Diego Rivera (1886–1957), José Clemente Orozco (1883–1949), and David Alfaro Siqueiros (1896-1974). It has also hosted, in the past few years, highly praised exhibitions of national and international modern art.

Museo Mural Diego Rivera: Diego Rivera's famous mural Dream of a Sunday Afternoon in Alameda Park was transferred here after the 1985 earthquake destroyed its original home, the Hotel Prado. Across 50 feet and in vibrant colors, Rivera portrays almost all of the most important figures in the city's history—including a self-portrait of himself as a boy, and his wife, Frida Kahlo.

Museo de Arte Popular: Dedicated to Mexican folk art, the museum is a dazzler, showcasing everything from Huichol yarn paintings to Tecali glasswork.

In Mexico City, there were/are countless world class restaurants and frankly some of these match or are even better than the top places in Paris, London, New York etc

The top three for me are La fondo Del recuerdo, Del Lago and Churchill. If life gives any one the opportunity to visit Mexico City then I strongly recommend a visit to all these three places. All very different but each of them has unique features giving an extraordinary experience each time one visits these world class restuarants. La fondo de recuerdo is a great way to be introduced to the Mexican cuisines and has a cultural ambience. Del Lago in the middle of the Chaupltepec Park is an elegant place perhaps a romantic spot offering a wonderful dining experience. Churchill is an English themed restaurant with the very authentic décor located in the heart of the posh Polanco district. It was an English mansion that was transformed into this restaurant. The specialities are based on beef and some are very English recipes.

The main meal to enjoy at the best of these places was lunch rather than dinner and this was very much related to the business ethics but it was also very popular with social get togethers. A typical lunch would be to meet at the restaurant by 13.00 hours and start getting into the cocktails with light bites. Around 14.00 hours the formal starter dishes were ordered and wine appeared on the scene. I am not going to start discussing Mexican wines because these are of a fine quality both white and red. Most of these wines are a legacy of the Spanish rule, with the earliest vineyards attributed to the Monasteries. Returning back to the lunch things got really warm by 15.00 hours and then the Menu was sought to choose the main course! this duly arrived by 15.30 or so .Given the break after the main course with more wine the dessert arrived around 16.30 followed by some fine local liqueurs (the finest Tequila and Kahlau often featured) and the International offerings. The final toast would be drunk around 17.30 and then we all went back to the office!!!

There are so many places to visit in Mexico and each place has something unique to offer. Even in the prolonged stay I could not visit every place that I wanted to visit in that country. Of all the regrets, I really did want to visit Baja California but never made it. This State is famous for a unique geographical lay out and wonderful beaches. This meant that I never did visit the legendary border town of Tijuana and the famous resort of Cabo San Lucas. Perhaps, one day I shall make it.

I did visit Neuvo Laredo connecting Mexico to the State of Texas in the USA. It is fascinating watching the amount of human movement across the various check points. How this could be brought down, I do not know. Each border town between the two countries has an element of tension and thus Neuvo Laredo was not a relaxing environment. Perception is indeed reality

Guadalajara - Guadalajara is the cultural center of western Mexico and the second most important city in the country. Cultural tourism is one of the most important economic activities, especially in the historic centres.

The Guadalajara cuisine is a mix of pre-Hispanic and Spanish influences, like the rest of Mexico, but dishes have their own flavors and are made with local techniques.

One of the main distinguishing dishes is birria. This is goat or lamb meat cooked in a spicy sauce seasoned with chili peppers, ginger, cumin, black pepper, oregano and cloves. The traditional way of preparing birria is to pit roast the meat and spices wrapped in maguey leaves. It is served in bowls with minced onion, limes and tortillas.

Another dish that is strongly associated with Guadalajara is tortas ahogadas, literally "drowned tortas (sub sandwiches)." This sandwich is an oblong "bolillo" bun filled with pork and other ingredients. Then the sandwich is covered in a red tomato/chili pepper sauce.

Vera Cruz – Of course this city was my motivation to travel and get to Mexico so it will always hold a place in my heart. The city has great a History in terms of Spanish Conquistadors who set up this place.

Perhaps not the best tourist place but has character and historical traditions.

Veracruz has a blend of cultures, mostly indigenous, ethnic Spanish and Afro-Cuban. The influence of these three is best seen in the food and music of the area, which has strong Spanish, Caribbean and African influences.

Fortin de las Flores – While working around the state of Vera Cruz I discovered this quaint little town which had a beautiful town square with a standout cathedral. It offered some unique small hotels and the weather was often temperate

Volcano Popcatepetl – Every time that I flew to and from Mexico City to Villahermosa the site of Popcatepetl was fascinating. There cannot be many views from an Aeroplane window.  This is a live volcano with an altitude of 17,000 feet. There a many legends associated with it. The view that adorns the world's largest city – Mexico City – is enhanced by the majesty of two of the highest volcanoes in the hemisphere: Popocatepetl and Iztaccíhuatl. Both of these volcanoes are named after ancient lovers. As most of the great love stories go these also had a tragic end.

A mural depicting the story of the two lovers.

Popocatepetl

Acapulco – The resort whose name was associated with the early era of Hollywood. Famous stars of yester years like John Wayne, Johnny Wesimuller , Elvis Presley etc frequented the place. The Acapulco Princess hotel and its sister property Pierre Marques hosted the world famous people.

The economy grew and foreign investment increased with it. During the 1950s, Acapulco became the fashionable place for millionaire Hollywood stars such as Elizabeth Taylor, Frank Sinatra, Eddie Fisher and Brigitte Bardot

During the 1960s and 1970s, new hotel resorts were built, and accommodation and transport were made cheaper. It was no longer necessary to be a millionaire to spend a holiday in Acapulco; the foreign and Mexican middle class could now afford to travel here. However, as more hotels were built in the south part of the bay, the old hotels of the 1950s lost their grandeur.

The famous Cliff divers of La Quebrada

During the 1990s, the road known as the Ruta del Sol was built, crossing the mountains between Mexico City and Acapulco. The journey takes only about three and a half hours, making Acapulco a favorite weekend destination for Mexico City inhabitants. It was in that time period that the economic impact of Acapulco as a tourist destination increased.

The port continued to grow and in 1996, a new private company, API Acapulco, was created to manage operations. This consolidated operations and now Acapulco is the major port for car exports to the Pacific.

In the 2000s, the drug war in Mexico has had a negative effect on tourism in Acapulco as rival drug traffickers fight each other for the Guerrero coast route that brings drugs from South America as well as soldiers that have been fighting the cartels since 2006. A major gun battle between 18 gunmen and soldiers took place in the summer of 2009 in the Old Acapulco seaside area, lasting hours and killing 16 of the gunmen and two soldiers. This came after the swine flu outbreak earlier in the year nearly paralyzed the Mexican economy, forcing hotels to give discounts to bring tourists back. One hopes that the resort can recover its previous popularity.

ACAPULCO PRINCESS AND THE PIERRE MARQUES HOTELS

Puerto Vallarta – A beautiful resort on the Pacific side of Mexico. Made famous by the filming of the famous Richard Burton Movie 'The night of the Iguana' in the 60s. A wonderful resort. Many leisure cruises make it a stop for their passengers and in the 80's and 90s this resort was very popular with the Cruise liner associated with the TV series 'The Love Boat.

Cancun – Cancún, a Mexican city on the Yucatán Peninsula bordering the Caribbean Sea, is known for its beaches, numerous resorts and nightlife. It's composed of 2 distinct areas: the more traditional downtown area, El Centro, and

Zona Hotelera, a long, beachfront strip of high-rise hotels, nightclubs, shops and restaurants. Cancun is also a famed destination for students during universities' spring break period.

Cuernavaca – Cuernavaca was nicknamed "city of eternal spring" by Alexander von Humboldt in the 19th century.The city is located in a tropical region, but its temperature is kept fairly constant in the 70s (°F). It is located on the southern slope of the Sierra de Chichinautzin Mountains. In the morning, warm air flows up the mountains from the valley below and in the late afternoon, cooler air flows down from the higher elevations. A ubiquitous flowering plant in the city is the bougainvillea.

Taxco - Taxco de Alarcón (usually referred to as simply Taxco) is a small city and administrative center of a Taxco de Alarcón Municipality located in the Mexican state of Guerrero. Taxco is located in the north-central part of the state, (106 miles) southwest of Mexico City and a wonderful weekend getaway location

The city is heavily associated with silver, both with the mining of it and other metals and for the crafting of it into jewelry, silverware and other items. Today, mining is no longer a mainstay of the city's economy. The city's reputation for silverwork, along with its picturesque homes and surrounding landscapes, have made tourism the main economic activity.

There are many other interesting places to visit e.g Guajanuato – lovely surrondings but a bit morbid with its 'Mummy' Museum.The city of Catemaco rumoured to be associated with witch craft

The two other places all beginning with an M also offer unique attractions, being sea side resorts: Mazatalan and Manzanillo.


## MEXICAN MUSIC

The music of Mexico is very diverse and features a wide range of musical genres and performance styles. It has been influenced by a variety of cultures, most notably indigenous peoples of Mexico and Europe.

The Mariachi band consisting of five people is most notably associated with Mexico. It is a part of life and tradition and amongst others if you want to give a loved one a surprise on their birthday, you wake them at 05.00 hrs with a Mariachi band and a full scale gathering of friends and families. It is a bit early to get on the Cuba Libres but what the heck, most of the neighbourhood joins in sooner or later.

For me the most haunting and soul touching music was the derivative of the Cuban Bolero. I challenge anyone to listen to the compilations by the Mejor Compania and the Pequena Compania and not be impressed. I might be wrong in saying but the Mexican Music is the beacon for the Latin American musicians to base most of their work on.

Of course who can forget the unforgettable sounds of Santana from 1966 onwards!


HISTORY OF MEXICO

The history of Mexico is fascinating; Mexico was home to many advanced ancient civilizations, such as the Olmec, Toltec, Teotihuacan, Zapotec, Maya and Aztec and each era has left historical landmarks in the country. In 1521, the Spanish Empire conquered and colonized the territory. In 1821 after the Mexican War of Independence the country gained its independence. The tumultuous post-independence period was characterized by economic instability and many political changes. The Mexican–American War (1846–48) led to the territorial cession of the extensive northern borderlands, one-third of its territory, to the United States. The Pastry War, the Franco-Mexican War, a civil war, two empires and a domestic dictatorship occurred through the 19th century. The dictatorship was overthrown in the Mexican Revolution of 1910, which culminated with the promulgation of the 1917 Constitution and the emergence of the country's current political system.

In 1929, Calles founded the National Revolutionary Party (PNR), later renamed the Institutional Revolutionary Party (PRI), and started a period known as the

Maximato, which ended with the election of Lázaro Cárdenas, who implemented many economic and social reforms. This included the Mexican oil expropriation in March 1938, which nationalized the U.S. and Anglo-Dutch oil company known as the Mexican Eagle Petroleum Company. This movement would result in the creation of the state-owned Mexican oil company known as Pemex. This sparked a diplomatic crisis with the countries whose citizens had lost businesses by Cárdenas' radical measure, but since then the company has played an important role in the economic development of Mexico.

Between 1940 and 1980, Mexico remained a poor country but experienced substantial economic growth that some historians call the "Mexican miracle".Although the economy continued to flourish for some, social inequality remained a factor of discontent. Moreover, the PRI rule became increasingly authoritarian and at times oppressive.

February, 1982

A sharp decline in international reserves forces the Mexican government to devaluate the peso, increasing the dollar-denominated debt burden, mainly to US commercial banks (Figures 1 and 2). Despite the devaluation of the peso, Mexico is unable to stop its loss of reserves and runs out of cash. International reserves are only sufficient to cover three weeks' of imports.

August 12th, 1982

Mexico's Minister of Finance Silva Hertog informs the US government and the IMF that Mexico is unable to service its external debt of USD 80bn (FDIC, 1997).

September 1st, 1982

The government nationalizes Mexico's private banking system in order to prevent bankruptcy of the private banking sector and imposes comprehensive exchange controls. In the following months, a de facto moratorium on debt service exists. All payments on the private sector debt cease, as well as most payments on the principal of the public sector debt (Buffie, 1989).

Aftermath

In August 1982, western central banks, at the behest of the US government and Federal Reserve Chairman Paul Volcker, arrange an unprecedented USD 1.5bn loan to Mexico, additional to USD 2bn in cash (oil prepayments and agricultural credits) from the US government. In essence, Mexico receives USD 3.5bn to relieve immediate cash needs, but only a 90-day rollover of the principal (Goldman, 1982).

Figure 1: Exchange rate

Figure 1: Exchange rate Source: EIU

Figure 2: External debt burden

Figure 2: External debt burdenSource: World Bank

In December 1982, the IMF approves a USD 3.8bn loan to the Mexican government. As a condition, the government has to implement a series of free market reforms. The IMF program ended in December 1985. Two more programs lasted from 1986 to 1988 and from 1989 to 1993. The programs together amounted to 5.2% of GDP (Barkbu, 2011).

Between August and December 1982, the peso is devaluated nearly 50% again the US dollar. Consequently, elevated inflation rates reach 100% and the economy turns into a recession. In 1982, the economy shrinks by 0.6%, followed by a shrink of 4.2% in 1983. Real GDP per capita falls with respectively 3% and 6% in 1982 and 1983. During the following five years, it decreases by 11% in total. In the same period, real wages fall by approximately 30% (Buffie 1989). Unemployment increases to high levels, especially in rural areas. In 1982, contractions in investment and consumption negatively contributed to economic growth (see figure 3).

Figure 3: Decomposition of economic growth

Figure 3: Decomposition of economic growth

Source: OECD

After the devaluation of the peso in February 1982, net exports sharply increase, the only positive contributor to growth. In the five years after the crisis, Mexico's terms of trade declined by 42.2%. But at the end of 1986, Mexico is still saddled with a huge foreign debt amounting to 78% of GDP and inflation exceeds 100%. In the same year, world market oil prices collapsed, adversely impacting the economy's economic performance. Between 1983 and 1988, Mexico's real GDP grew at an average rate of just 0.1% per year. Therefore, the 80s are considered to be the "lost decade".

Short economic history

From the mid-1950s to the beginning of the 1970s, Mexico enjoyed a period of macroeconomic stability and economic growth. The inflation rate never exceeded, while annual economic growth averaged 7%. From 1954 to 1976, Mexico had a fixed exchange rate regime. The peso was fixed to the US dollar at 12.5 peso per dollar (see Figure 1).

In 1970, Mexico's economic policy changed radically when Luis Echeverria was inaugurated as president. An enormous fiscal expansion took place and public debt started to increase. Consequently, budget deficits soared to 10% of GDP in 1975 and 1976. The growth rate of the monetary base accelerated to 33.8% in 1975. Consequently, inflation rose above 20% in 1973 and 1974. Meanwhile, the balance of payments deteriorated. Due to rising inflation, the real exchange rate appreciated rapidly and was largely overvalued. The current account deficit recorded 5% of GDP in 1975. Total foreign debt increased sharply to 31% of GDP in 1976. Almost all of this debt was held by the public sector, lent by international commercial banks (Buffie, 1989). Approximately three-quarters of the interest payments were tied to US interest rates and the London Interbank Offering Rate (LIBOR), which repriced every six months. Therefore, these credits were especially vulnerable to repricing risk driven by changes in the macroeconomic conditions of the creditor nations.

On 31 august 1976, under huge balance of payments pressure, the peso devaluated nearly 50% and the economy turned into a recession. Shortly thereafter, Lopez Portillo was installed as president. He reached an agreement with the IMF on a stabilization program. In the first year, inflation, the current account deficit and the budget deficit started to fall.


1979 - 1982: The run up to the crisis

Following the start of the production of newly discovered oil reserves in 1979, the IMF program was dropped and a more expansionary fiscal policy was implemented. Between 1978 and 1981, real GDP growth varied between 8.0 and 9.1%. The inflation rate accelerated but did not exceed 30%.

Since 1979, several factors worsened the debt service burden. When the second oil shock occurred in 1979, oil prices skyrocketed. This was favorable for Mexico as oil exporter, as it increased oil revenues. However, the following worldwide recession was a major negative factor, lowering net exports. In the same year, worldwide interest rates reached record levels. The increase in US interest rates was caused by the Federal Reserve's policy to curb the oil-based inflation of the 1970s. This resulted in rising US dollar exchange rates, increasing the difficulty of servicing debt. Compounding this, as about three-quarters of interest payments were tied to variable interest rates, debt service payments increased and made debt repayment more difficult.  In 1981, LIBOR peaked at 16.7% on average, before lowering to 13.6% in 1982.

Figure 4: Change in international reserves

Figure 4: Change in international reserves

Source: Banco de México

Another feature was the overvalued exchange rate of the peso. From mid-1978 to mid-1980, the nominal exchange rate was held constant, even though annual inflation exceeded 20%. The resulting overvalued exchange rate generated fears of devaluation, leading to more capital flight. Nevertheless, heavy borrowing continued (FDIC, 1997). From mid-1980 to early1982, the peso gradually depreciated 16%, while annual inflation recorded nearly 30%. As a result, the real exchange rate appreciated steadily. The real interest rate turned negative, further stimulating debt accumulation. In early 1982 the peso was left to float freely until June 1982. Consequently, the peso depreciated around 50%. However, this was not enough to end overvaluation. Nevertheless, it was a sudden worsening of the terms of trade, decreasing by 13% in 1982. Increased financial instability and prospects of further devaluations stimulated further capital flight. The weak government response around the elections in 1982 raised uncertainty and aggravated the situation. In 1981 and 1982 capital flight was estimated at respectively 3.4% and 4.2% of GDP.

In 1980, government expenditures escalated, resulting in large fiscal deficits, since it was not matched by a similar rise in revenues. Non-oil revenues even decreased, principally due to the government's reluctance to raise administered prices (Buffie, 1989). The budget deficit grew steadily to 14.7% in 1981. Public debt recorded 42% of GDP that year, while external debt had already increased to 33% of GDP. After the devaluations of the peso and rising global interest rates, Mexico's external debt reached 49% of GDP in 1982 (see Figure 1). Debt service absorbed 142% of total current account income and 24% of GDP (Buffie, 1989). As a result, in August 1982, Mexico was no longer able to service its external debt.

Debt restructuring

In 1982, the government began with a two-year respite from large scale debt service payments, granted by US commercial banks. On 10 December 1982, an agreement was reached with the commercial banks to reschedule USD 23bn of capital payments on the public sector debt coming due between 23 August 1982 and 31 December 1984. During the same period a wide-ranging stabilization program was agreed with the IMF. The program also included structural reforms.

At the time of the Mexican default, debt often exceeded the capital base of many of international banks. Therefore, many feared that the banking system would collapse.

In the face of falling economic growth rates and rising inflation, the "Baker plan" was implemented in 1982, proposed by US Treasury secretary Baker (van Wijnbergen, 1991). In return for economic reforms, high-debt countries would get new access to medium-term new loans, in addition to rolling over of amortization of old loans. New loans had to come both from commercial creditors and the official lending institutions. In June 1983, the "Paris Club", representing creditor governments, rescheduled Mexico's sovereign debt owed to major creditor countries (World Bank, 2004). The Paris Club is an informal group of financial officials from most western economies, which provides financial services such as debt restructuring and debt relief. With access to capital markets restored, it was hoped that the economic reforms would allow the debtors to grow out of debt. However, capital outflows went up rather than down, inflation skyrocketed, investment fell and over the period 1982-1988, no economic growth took place in Mexico at all. Consequently, external debt rose to 78% of GDP in 1987, marking the failure of the "Baker Plan".

In September 1989, the "Brady plan" was agreed, legitimizing the concept of debt relief. By now, it was believed that US banks could withstand projected losses on Latin American debt (Tammen, 1990). The "Brady Plan" forced them to do so. The basic idea was to make debt relief acceptable to commercial bank creditors by offering a smaller but much safer payment stream in exchange for the original claim that clearly could not be serviced in full (FDIC). The Mexican government and the Bank Advisory Committee representing the commercial bank creditors reached an agreement on a financing package covering the period 1989-92, restructuring approximately USD 49.8bn of Mexico's external debt. As only long-term debt with commercial banks was restructured, roughly half of the debt was involved (van Wijnbergen, 1991). Commercial banks involved had three options (Odubekun, 2005):

Banks could exchange old loans for new bonds at a discount of 35% of their face value, keeping interest rates at market levels (equivalent to LIBOR + %)

Banks could exchange old debt for face-value new bonds (called par bonds) bearing fixed interest rates of 6.25%

Banks could provide additional loans over the next three years equivalent to 25% of the banks' initial medium- and long-term loans, which implied no debt relief but the provision of new money

Most banks opted for the par bond (47%), implying interest rate reduction. Other banks chose to reduce the principal (40%), a few offered new loans (13%). Another agreement was reached with the Paris Club, representing creditor governments, covering USD 2.6bn of principal and interest payments falling due in the period 1989-1992 (van Wijnbergen, 1991).

The "Brady plan" substantially improved Mexico's ability to service its external debt by reducing interest and principal payments (Dornbusch, 1994).


Structural reforms

In December 1982, Mexico started far-reaching structural reforms, which were a condition for receiving the IMF loan. The reforms included: fiscal austerity, privatization of state-owned companies, reductions in trade barriers, industrial deregulation, and foreign investment liberalization. Owing to rigidly enforced fiscal discipline, the budget deficit halved from 17.6% in 1982 to 8.9% in 1983. Fiscal austerity was accompanied by stringent monetary policy.

With an extensive trade reform, Mexico opened up the economy. The percentage of domestic (non-oil) tradable production covered by import quotas was lowered from 100% in 1984 to less than 20% in 1991. Also, maximum import tariffs were cut. As a result, non-oil merchandise exports doubled their share of total exports to two-thirds. In May 1989, foreign investment regulations were considerably relaxed and made more transparent.

Also the tax system underwent a number of reforms, encouraging capital inflows and raising sanctions for tax evasion. The government also initiated a process of financial market liberalization. Ceilings on commercial banks' deposit interest rates were removed. Forced allocation of commercial credit towards favored sectors had also been abolished and credit subsidies through official development banks had been reduced. In 1991, Mexico started to privatize the commercial banks, which were nationalized in 1982. However, banking sector reforms were delayed. Mexico still lacked inadequate banking sector supervision, although the government guaranteed both deposits and liabilities. See Special Report 2013/15: The Tequila crisis in 1994.

Conclusion

In August 1982, Mexico was not able to service its external debt obligations, marking the start of the debt crisis. After years of accumulating external debt, risen world interest rates, the worldwide recession and sudden devaluations of the peso caused external debt payments to rise sharply. Since November 1982, several forms of debt restructuring were applied, including the Baker plan and Brady plan. Under the Brady plan, US banks assumed the losses on Mexican debt. The IMF assisted with three financial packages, which were accompanied by structural reforms.

In the 1980s the first cracks emerged in PRI's monopolistic position. In Baja California, Ernesto Ruffo Appel was elected as governor. In 1988, alleged electoral fraud prevented the leftist candidate Cuauhtémoc Cárdenas from winning the national presidential elections, giving Carlos Salinas de Gortari the presidency and leading to massive protests in Mexico City.

Salinas embarked on a program of neoliberal reforms which fixed the exchange rate, controlled inflation and culminated with the signing of the North American Free Trade Agreement (NAFTA), which came into effect on January 1, 1994. The same day, the Zapatista Army of National Liberation (EZLN) started a two-week-long armed rebellion against the federal government, and has continued as a non-violent opposition movement against neoliberalism and globalization.

From the mid-1950s to the beginning of the 1970s, Mexico enjoyed a period of macroeconomic stability and economic growth. The inflation rate never exceeded, while annual economic growth averaged 7%. From 1954 to 1976, Mexico had a fixed exchange rate regime. The peso was fixed to the US dollar at 12.5 peso per dollar (see Figure 1).

In 1970, Mexico's economic policy changed radically when Luis Echeverria was inaugurated as president. An enormous fiscal expansion took place and public debt started to increase. Consequently, budget deficits soared to 10% of GDP in 1975 and 1976. The growth rate of the monetary base accelerated to 33.8% in 1975. Consequently, inflation rose above 20% in 1973 and 1974. Meanwhile, the balance of payments deteriorated. Due to rising inflation, the real exchange rate appreciated rapidly and was largely overvalued. The current account deficit recorded 5% of GDP in 1975. Total foreign debt increased sharply to 31% of GDP in 1976. Almost all of this debt was held by the public sector, lent by international commercial banks (Buffie, 1989). Approximately three-quarters of the interest payments were tied to US interest rates and the London Interbank Offering Rate (LIBOR), which repriced every six months. Therefore, these credits were especially vulnerable to repricing risk driven by changes in the macroeconomic conditions of the creditor nations.

On 31 august 1976, under huge balance of payments pressure, the peso devaluated nearly 50% and the economy turned into a recession. Shortly thereafter, Lopez Portillo was installed as president. He reached an agreement with the IMF on a stabilization program. In the first year, inflation, the current account deficit and the budget deficit started to fall.

1979 - 1982: The run up to the crisis

Following the start of the production of newly discovered oil reserves in 1979, the IMF program was dropped and a more expansionary fiscal policy was implemented. Between 1978 and 1981, real GDP growth varied between 8.0 and 9.1%. The inflation rate accelerated but did not exceed 30%.

Since 1979, several factors worsened the debt service burden. When the second oil shock occurred in 1979, oil prices skyrocketed. This was favorable for Mexico as oil exporter, as it increased oil revenues. However, the following worldwide recession was a major negative factor, lowering net exports. In the same year, worldwide interest rates reached record levels. The increase in US interest rates was caused by the Federal Reserve's policy to curb the oil-based inflation of the 1970s. This resulted in rising US dollar exchange rates, increasing the difficulty of servicing debt. Compounding this, as about three-quarters of interest payments were tied to variable interest rates, debt service payments increased and made debt repayment more difficult.  In 1981, LIBOR peaked at 16.7% on average, before lowering to 13.6% in 1982.

Figure 4: Change in international reserves

Figure 4: Change in international reserves


Source: Banco de México

Another feature was the overvalued exchange rate of the peso. From mid-1978 to mid-1980, the nominal exchange rate was held constant, even though annual inflation exceeded 20%. The resulting overvalued exchange rate generated fears of devaluation, leading to more capital flight. Nevertheless, heavy borrowing continued (FDIC, 1997). From mid-1980 to early1982, the peso gradually depreciated 16%, while annual inflation recorded nearly 30%. As a result, the real exchange rate appreciated steadily. The real interest rate turned negative, further stimulating debt accumulation. In early 1982 the peso was left to float freely until June 1982. Consequently, the peso depreciated around 50%. However, this was not enough to end overvaluation. Nevertheless, it was a sudden worsening of the terms of trade, decreasing by 13% in 1982. Increased financial instability and prospects of further devaluations stimulated further capital flight. The weak government response around the elections in 1982 raised uncertainty and aggravated the situation. In 1981 and 1982 capital flight was estimated at respectively 3.4% and 4.2% of GDP.

In 1980, government expenditures escalated, resulting in large fiscal deficits, since it was not matched by a similar rise in revenues. Non-oil revenues even decreased, principally due to the government's reluctance to raise administered prices (Buffie, 1989). The budget deficit grew steadily to 14.7% in 1981. Public debt recorded 42% of GDP that year, while external debt had already increased to 33% of GDP. After the devaluations of the peso and rising global interest rates, Mexico's external debt reached 49% of GDP in 1982 (see Figure 1). Debt service absorbed 142% of total current account income and 24% of GDP (Buffie, 1989). As a result, in August 1982, Mexico was no longer able to service its external debt.

Debt restructuring

In 1982, the government began with a two-year respite from large scale debt service payments, granted by US commercial banks. On 10 December 1982, an agreement was reached with the commercial banks to reschedule USD 23bn of capital payments on the public sector debt coming due between 23 August 1982 and 31 December 1984. During the same period a wide-ranging stabilization program was agreed with the IMF. The program also included structural reforms.

At the time of the Mexican default, debt often exceeded the capital base of many of international banks. Therefore, many feared that the banking system would collapse.

In the face of falling economic growth rates and rising inflation, the "Baker plan" was implemented in 1982, proposed by US Treasury secretary Baker (van Wijnbergen, 1991). In return for economic reforms, high-debt countries would get new access to medium-term new loans, in addition to rolling over of amortization of old loans. New loans had to come both from commercial creditors and the official lending institutions. In June 1983, the "Paris Club", representing creditor governments, rescheduled Mexico's sovereign debt owed to major creditor countries (World Bank, 2004). The Paris Club is an informal group of financial officials from most western economies, which provides financial services such as debt restructuring and debt relief. With access to capital markets restored, it was hoped that the economic reforms would allow the debtors to grow out of debt. However, capital outflows went up rather than down, inflation skyrocketed, investment fell and over the period 1982-1988, no economic growth took place in Mexico at all. Consequently, external debt rose to 78% of GDP in 1987, marking the failure of the "Baker Plan".

In September 1989, the "Brady plan" was agreed, legitimizing the concept of debt relief. By now, it was believed that US banks could withstand projected losses on Latin American debt (Tammen, 1990). The "Brady Plan" forced them to do so. The basic idea was to make debt relief acceptable to commercial bank creditors by offering a smaller but much safer payment stream in exchange for the original claim that clearly could not be serviced in full (FDIC). The Mexican government and the Bank Advisory Committee representing the commercial bank creditors reached an agreement on a financing package covering the period 1989-92, restructuring approximately USD 49.8bn of Mexico's external debt. As only long-term debt with commercial banks was restructured, roughly half of the debt was involved (van Wijnbergen, 1991). Commercial banks involved had three options (Odubekun, 2005):

Banks could exchange old loans for new bonds at a discount of 35% of their face value, keeping interest rates at market levels (equivalent to LIBOR + %)

Banks could exchange old debt for face-value new bonds (called par bonds) bearing fixed interest rates of 6.25%

Banks could provide additional loans over the next three years equivalent to 25% of the banks' initial medium- and long-term loans, which implied no debt relief but the provision of new money

Most banks opted for the par bond (47%), implying interest rate reduction. Other banks chose to reduce the principal (40%), a few offered new loans (13%). Another agreement was reached with the Paris Club, representing creditor governments, covering USD 2.6bn of principal and interest payments falling due in the period 1989-1992 (van Wijnbergen, 1991).

The "Brady plan" substantially improved Mexico's ability to service its external debt by reducing interest and principal payments (Dornbusch, 1994).


Structural reforms

In December 1982, Mexico started far-reaching structural reforms, which were a condition for receiving the IMF loan. The reforms included: fiscal austerity, privatization of state-owned companies, reductions in trade barriers, industrial deregulation, and foreign investment liberalization. Owing to rigidly enforced fiscal discipline, the budget deficit halved from 17.6% in 1982 to 8.9% in 1983. Fiscal austerity was accompanied by stringent monetary policy.

With an extensive trade reform, Mexico opened up the economy. The percentage of domestic (non-oil) tradable production covered by import quotas was lowered from 100% in 1984 to less than 20% in 1991. Also, maximum import tariffs were cut. As a result, non-oil merchandise exports doubled their share of total exports to two-thirds. In May 1989, foreign investment regulations were considerably relaxed and made more transparent.

Also the tax system underwent a number of reforms, encouraging capital inflows and raising sanctions for tax evasion. The government also initiated a process of financial market liberalization. Ceilings on commercial banks' deposit interest rates were removed. Forced allocation of commercial credit towards favored sectors had also been abolished and credit subsidies through official development banks had been reduced. In 1991, Mexico started to privatize the commercial banks, which were nationalized in 1982. However, banking sector reforms were delayed. Mexico still lacked inadequate banking sector supervision, although the government guaranteed both deposits and liabilities. See Special Report 2013/15: The Tequila crisis in 1994.

In August 1982, Mexico was not able to service its external debt obligations, marking the start of the debt crisis. After years of accumulating external debt, risen world interest rates, the worldwide recession and sudden devaluations of the peso caused external debt payments to rise sharply. Since November 1982, several forms of debt restructuring were applied, including the Baker plan and Brady plan. Under the Brady plan, US banks assumed the losses on Mexican debt. The IMF assisted with three financial packages, which were accompanied by structural reforms.

In 1994, Salinas was succeeded by Ernesto Zedillo, followed by the Mexican peso crisis and a $50 billion IMF bailout. Major macroeconomic reforms were started by President Zedillo, and the economy rapidly recovered and growth peaked at almost 7% by the end of 1999.

Mexico has the fifteenth largest nominal GDP and the eleventh largest by purchasing power parity. The Mexican economy is strongly linked to those of its North American Free Trade Agreement (NAFTA) partners, especially the United States.[16][17] Mexico was the first Latin American member of the Organisation for Economic Co-operation and Development (OECD), joining in 1994. It is classified as an upper-middle income country by the World Bank and a newly industrialized country by several analysts. By 2050, Mexico could become the world's fifth or seventh largest economy. The country is considered both a regional power and middle power, and is often identified as an emerging global power. Due to its rich culture and history, Mexico ranks first in the Americas and seventh in the world by number of UNESCO World Heritage Sites. Mexico is a mega diverse country, ranking fourth in the world by biodiversity. In 2015 it was the 9th most visited country in the world, with 32.1 million international arrivals. Mexico is a member of the United Nations, the World Trade Organization, the G8+5, the G20, the Uniting for Consensus and the Pacific Alliance.

Mexico City hosted the XIX Olympic Games in 1968, making it the first Latin American city to do so. The country has also hosted the FIFA World Cup twice, in 1970 and 1986.

MEXICAN FOOD

Part of the fascination for this country is created by its food! Various cuisines and the manner and style of eating add to the pleasure.

Mexican cuisine is as complex as any other world cuisine, such as those of China, France, Italy and Japan. It is created mostly with ingredients native to Mexico, as well as those brought over by the Spanish conquistadors, with some new influences since then. In addition to staples, such as corn and chile peppers, native ingredients include tomatoes, squashes, avocados, cocoa and vanilla, as well as ingredients not generally used in other cuisines, such as edible flowers, vegetables like huauzontle and papaloquelite, or small criollo avocados, whose skin is edible.

Vegetables play an important role in Mexican cuisine. Common vegetables include zucchini, cauliflower, corn, potatoes, spinach, swiss chard, mushrooms, jitomate (red tomato), green tomato, etc. Other traditional vegetable dishes include chile rellenos, huitlacoche (corn fungus), huauzontle, and nopalitos (cactus leaves) to name a few.

European contributions include pork, chicken, beef, cheese, herbs and spices, as well as some fruits. Tropical fruits such as guava, prickly pear, sapote, mangoes, bananas, pineapple and cherimoya (custard apple) are popular, especially in the center and south of the country. It has been debated how much Mexican food is still indigenous and how much is European.[9] However, the basis of the diet is still corn and beans, with chilli pepper as a seasoning, as they are complementary foods.

Despite the introduction of wheat and rice to Mexico, the basic starch remains corn in almost all areas of the country. While it is eaten fresh, most corn is dried, treated with lime and ground into a dough called masa.This dough is used both fresh and fermented to make a wide variety of dishes from drinks (atole, pozol, etc.) to tamales, sopas, and much more. However, the most common way to eat corn in Mexico is in the form of a tortilla, which accompanies almost every dish. Tortillas are made of corn in most of the country, but other versions exist, such as wheat in the north or plantain, yuca and wild greens in Oaxaca.

Chili peppers - A molcajete and tejolote, the traditional mortar and pestle of Mexico.

The other basic ingredient in all parts of Mexico is the chili pepper. Mexican food has a reputation for being very spicy, but its seasoning can be better described as strong. Many dishes also have subtle flavors. Chilis are used for their flavors and not just their heat, with Mexico using the widest variety. If a savory dish or snack does not contain chili pepper, hot sauce is usually added, and chili pepper is often added to fresh fruit and sweets.

The importance of the Chili goes back to the Mesoamerican period, where it was considered to be as much of a staple as corn and beans. In the 16th century, Bartolomé de las Casas wrote that without chilis, the indigenous people did not think they were eating. Even today, most Mexicans believe that their national identity would be at a loss without chilis. In fact the symbol for the Football World cup 1986 was a chili!

Many dishes in Mexico are defined by their sauces and the chilis those sauces contain, rather than the meat or vegetable that the sauce covers. These dishes include entomatada (in tomato sauce), adobo or adobados, pipians and moles. A hominy soup called pozole is defined as white, green or red depending on the chili sauce used or omitted. Tamales are differentiated by the filling which is again defined by the sauce (red or green chili pepper strips or mole). Dishes without a sauce are rarely eaten without a salsa or without fresh or pickled chilis. This includes street foods, such as tacos, tortas, soups, sopes, tlacoyos, tlayudas, gorditas and sincronizadas. For most dishes, it is the type of chili used that gives it its main flavor.

Mexico's award-winning wines are offered at many restaurants, and the city offers unique experiences for tasting the regional spirits, with broad selections of Tequila and Mezcal. Mezcal is the drink with a worm resting peacefully at the bottom of the bottle. On many an occasion when the bottles are consumed with relative ease there can be races to see who gets to the worm first!!! There are many varieties of Tequila and some of these are of premium quality. Mexican wines have centuries old origins and although not known on the world stage are quality offering. Many of the vineyards were initiated by the missionaries coming from Spain

*Note: The memories of the 1985 earthquake mentioned in this section were once again brought to the fore as on exactly the same calendar day, 32 years later in 2017 an Earthquake of larger magnitude rocked Mexico city. This time the loss of life was smaller but still very tragic, the damage was intense but Mexico fought back again. In spite of the tragic outcome one has to recognize the mystical Mexico City and the spirit of its people.*

# AMAZING PERU

Who would not want to visit Peru?  So when I was asked at somewhat in the early stage of my career, I was on my way before the briefing was complete. I was to join a team of Engineers involved with the Commissioning and maintenance of 32 Gas Turbines on the Nor Peruano Crude oil pipeline. The base of our Company operations was in in the city of Piura some 1000 kms north of Lima. Enough briefing on the pipeline will follow in preceding sections

However, the main focus was to visit Machu Picchu famed throughout the world as the heritage sites of the ancient Incas. It was a privilege to visit Machu Picchu and at the time that I visited it was a four hour winding train journey from the elevated city of Cuzco. Mchu Picchu is a breath taking site and incredibly built in 1472 but abandoned a hundred years later by the Incas as the Spanish started to disturb their lives. It was hidden for a long time and discovered only in 1911 but there was evidence it had been plundered around 1870. Thus, it is 'not' the lost city of Incas having been abandoned by its own founders.

The famous El Condor Paso music theme rings in your ears as you arrive in Machu Picchu rendered by natives through many different musical instruments. Suffice

to say that this is one of the must Visit places for everyone at least once in their lives.

Lima is the capital of the country and an exciting metropolis offering everything to tourists. It is located on the Pacific coast. If I remember correctly, Miraflores was the area which had the best Hotel skyline, vibrating night spots and wonderful restaurants. I was more interested in discovering the northern part of the country, the Amazon territory.

I did take the time to visit another interesting place in Peru, Arequipa.In contrast to these other cities, Arequipa is an example of the Spanish and mestizo culture developed in Peru. There are no Inca artifacts or ruins in the city. In the winter it is warmer than in the summer. It is nicknamed the 'white city' (la ciudad blanca, in Spanish), because many of the buildings in the area are built of sillar, a white stone. This rock was quarried from the many volcanoes that surround the city, including the towering El Misti. Misti, Chachani and PichuPichu, are the three volcanoes surrounding the city. The only other place of note was Iquitos. As a city not accessible by road, motocycles and motocarros dominate unlike anywhere else.. This makes the city a bit more manic and loud. We had to travel and arrive in an Peruvian Air Force Float plane which takes off and lands on the river. The city has a disproportionate gender population split or was at the time. Men, especially foreigners were highly sought by groups of women especially in the evenings. It is the only place in the world that I have seen and experienced harassment by the opposite sex including being chased down an alleyway by a group of loud high spirited women. By the time I figured out that there was little point in running and why not be caught, the predators had given up. Sadly it never happened to me ever again. I sometimes wonder if it was a moment of fantasy!

I visited many other places in Peru but the main adventure lay in working in the pipeline and discovering the Amazons area and travel close to the border area with Brazil.

Peruvians are wonderful people, overwhelmingly kind and hospitable. I have to say that the ladies of Peru are very beautiful both on the outside and inside. That makes them very attractive and desirable to the opposite gender. On account of these wonderful people my time in Peru is one of the most cherished memories of my life.

Peru is known as the Gastronomical Centre of the Americas. A center of incorporated dishes brought by the conquistadors and waves of immigrants: African, European, Chinese and Japanese. Since the second half of the 20th century, international immigrants were joined by internal migrants from rural areas. Peruvian cuisines include Creole food, Chifas, Cebicherias and Pollerias. Although the Peruvian food remains virtually unknown in the Global gastronomic circles but it is one of the best in the world.

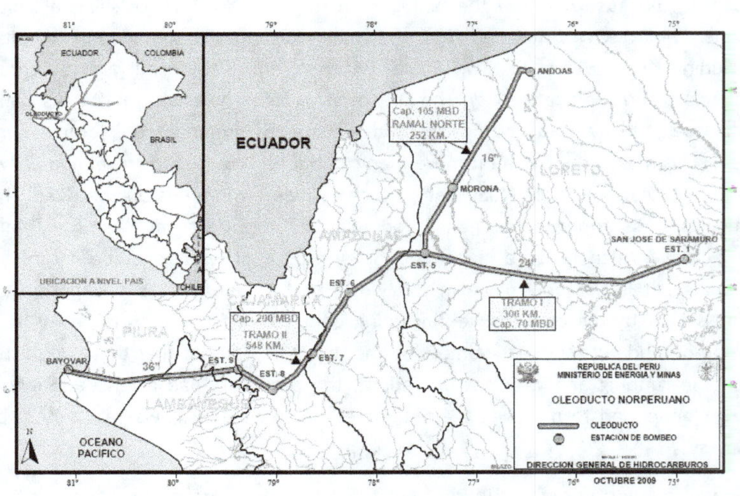


MAP 1 – STATION 5 – AMAZONAS AREA

The Norperuano pipeline is the longest pipeline in Peru. It was built in 1974 to transport oil from Loreto department across the Andes to the coast in Bayóvar, Piura department with a total of 1106 km to the west.

The pipeline begins in San José de Saramuro, in northeastern Peru. It arrives until Borja, where the north branch is united. The north branch crosses Moronda until arriving at Andoas. From Borja then it goes to Kuzu Grande, district of Manseriche until arriving at the coast in Bayóvar, department of Piura.

The Norperuano pipeline has a capacity of 100,000 barrels per day. The Peruvian state-owned company Petroperú was the operator of this pipeline.

History

The story began in 1972, when the government commissioned Petroperu, a subsidiary at that time of the Ministry of Energy and Mines, to carry out the studies required for the construction of the Norperuano Oil Pipeline and to make contracts with companies capable of carrying out such work.

The contract for the final design was awarded in 1973 to the firm Bechtel. On September 16, 1974, both parties signed it.

The laying of the first transport tubes required two years, with international participation.

On December 31, 1976, Station 1 of the Pipeline (San José de Saramuro) received oil from the Petroperu fields, and the first oil front arrived at Bayóvar Terminal on May 24, 1977. On June 7, Same year the tanker Trompeteros made the first shipment of crude oil to La Pampilla Refinery in Lima.

In the period of greatest activity, the construction of the Oil Pipeline demanded the effort of 7,800 workers - about a thousand of whom were foreigners.

Petroperú subsequently built the North Branch Pipeline, which runs from Andoas Station to Station 5. It entered operations on February 24, 1978.

Main Pipeline

The Norperuano Oil Pipeline begins with the collection of crude oil at Station 1, in San José de Saramuro (Loreto department), on the banks of the Marañón River and about 200 kilometers southeast of Iquitos.

The tubes advance westward, in the middle of the jungle, along the Marañón River, to Borja, where Station 5 is located, also a collection of crude oil.

Incidentally, I spent a lot of time at Station 5 and had the opportunity to explore the surrounding area and venture deep in the jungle by circumnavigating the river into the native territory

From this station, which is the point of convergence of the North Branch, the pipeline continues in a southeasterly direction to Station 6, in Kuzu Grande, district of Manseriche, province of Alto Amazonas. It continues parallel to the road that goes from Mesones Muro to Bagua, in the department of Amazonas, where Station 7 is located, and in a southeasterly direction it is reached to Station 8, in the vicinity of the district of Pucará, department of Cajamarca.

At that point, the pipeline changes to a northeasterly direction, to Station 9, which is the last pumping point, and from where it begins its ascent to the Andes mountain range, which crosses in the Paso de Porculla, at a maximum height Of 2,390 meters above sea level. In this place begins to descend until reaching the desert of the department of Piura, where rises the terminal of Bayóvar, in the bay of Sechura.


Pipeline North Branch

The North Branch Pipeline, with a length of 252 kilometers, was added in 1976 to the Norperuano Pipeline to make feasible transportation of the crude oil extracted from the Andoas oil fields.

It begins at the Andoas Station and continues westwards, crossing the Pastaza, Huazaga and Huituyacu rivers, where it changes from a southwesterly direction to the junction of the Morona River. In this place, is located the Pumping Station of Borja district, province of Alto Amazonas, department of Loreto.

Always in a south-westerly direction, it reaches the Marañón river, continues on flat and dry terrain to the Saramiriza river crossing, where the final route begins to Station 5 of the Main Pipeline.

Oleoaducto Ramal Norte was built by Grupo Mexicano Protexa in 1976, the main camp was located in Iquitos and auxiliary camps in the rivers Pataza and Marañon

The Norperuano Pipeline, has a length of 854 kilometers (crosses the coast, mountains and jungle). It is divided into two sections, the first of 306 kilometers, consisting of 24-inch diameter pipes connecting stations 1 and 5.

The North Branch has a length of 252 kilometers. It begins at the Andoas Station, converging at Station 5 with the main pipeline.

Some of the adventures worth narrating were in and around the pipeline. Station 1 was an hour's flight from Iquitos  and some details about the city are already documented. The main adventures were taking boat trips on the various rivers around the Amazon and visiting habitats of local tribes deep in the rain forests.

MAP 2 – IQUITOS – RIVER AMAZON

Some colleagues considered that I was mad to take such dangerous trips deep in the jungle risking life and more to the point jeopardizing my health. To me these were opportunities in life which could not possibly come again.

There was a member of Petro Peru staff who acted as a liaison for them with the local tribes. He was actually an off spring of a German explorer and a lady of the local indigenious Aguano tribe. He had blue eyes but dark hair and a light complexion. He was one of the finest people that I have ever met in my life. Everyone called him David although his real name was something else. He was a man of many skills when out on adventures, it was re-assuring to have him in close proximity especially when going into the unknown. Amongst other things he played the guitar very well and had a great voice and sang beautifully in whatever language took his fancy. He took to me as I was so much different to all the other foreigners working on the pipeline.

I joined him on many adventure trips in an around station 5 – Reference Map1 on the River Maranon into the Amazonas. Always taking a small boat carved out of logs fitted with a motor, lot of flasks of water, bottles of liquor and cases of beer. We were always accompanied by two tough security people armed with machetes and revolvers. Mostly these adventures were based on returning the same day although on a few occasions we returned quite late and travelling by a small boat in the early part of the night (albeit moonlit night) was pushing it a bit in the darkest jungles of Peru. A rainy night might have put paid to our adventures but somehow we escaped encountering a Tropical storm on all our sojourns.

Mostly, we arrived at small native settlements where David had contacts and went in to meet the elders of the village and pay respect for which we were treated with intense hospitality. We always took enough beer to spread it around so that as the attention of the hosts was diverted, I mostly got away without drinking or eating anything from whatever was offered by the hosts. However, it was not possible to do so every time and I had to at times swallow some very unmentionable items. At times after docking the boat we had to walk through the jungle on narrow paths for a few kilometres. The two security men had to at times hack way with the machetes to clear the way. These adventures were incredible experiences, entering the jungle you hear eerie sounds and a continuous shrilling sound followed by tweets etc.

I was always in a trance not believing that I was actually there, a very surreal experience. No matter how much Mosquito repellent I rubbed on such walks I was bitten beyond belief by all sorts of invisible 'things'. The clearing where the settlements were located were quite ok and I do not know what was done but I never really got bitten at those places. I was always wary of the horrible looking dogs with evil teeth, in fact they were not pure dogs but crosses between dogs and some other creatures???

The people were always friendly and very excited to see visitors especially one with a giant hooter and very different looking. The children of the village followed me everywhere and while in conversation with the elders there was always crowd of children, young women and even older women just staring at me. David always introduced me as a man from a faraway land, an Arab. Surprisingly, for people living in the remote places the wiser people knew about the outside world and talked about USA, the oceans, the crude Oil pipeline the construction of which had created many upheavals in their lives.

In that sort of environment sometimes I stopped to think and looked around me and saw human beings pretty much living their lives. Their homes may have been huts built with vegetation but always on stilts for protection from rain water and I dare say the creepy and crawlies etc some men were busy working on some small fields planting Yuca and some other local vegetables. Fish were hanging to be dried. Mothers were busy playing with their children or cleaning their huts. There was not much laughter but intensity of purpose.

As the day passed on, David always disappeared for his liaisons with his mistresses and he had at least one in every settlement we visited.

Before the sun really set a fire was always lit up in the centre of the settlement and it was a great sense of security in an otherwise dark surrounding. Even the horrible dogs became calmer as the blaze intensified and the whole ambience changed. More men seemed to return from the jungle after hunting for food with a variety of creatures and small boars.

Inevitably, David re-appeared to serenade everyone with the beer and liquor passed around.

During my visit to a settlement I discovered Masato!

In the rainforest of Peru, locals chew yuca and spit the masticated root into jars for fermentation. The resulting alcoholic beverage is a local staple called Masato. The Masato smells like pickle juice spiced with cloves.

As I arrived at the site the elders were busy 'producing Masato i.e. spitting with some intensity in this vessel. After welcoming me and much to my horror the jar/vessel was offered to me for a drink. Refusing a drink would have been social suicide in Amazonia, David looked pleadingly at me. With great courage I took a small sip. It tasted fruity, like sherry. Then I knocked back a bigger gulp, testing the murky drink with my tongue for any hint of saliva. Instead I came away with a cedar aftertaste. The jungle beverage was shockingly refreshing. Until today when I think of that moment I do not feel so good.

Masato, only one of its many names, is important for rainforest communities. The drink has been around for thousands of years. It's critical in everyday life as a source of carbohydrates, as a social lubricant and as a means of exerting political power, according to experts.

After gaining experience with these adventures, David and I took a trip on the river Amazon. From Station 1 we flew to Iquitos on Peruvian Air force float plane which lands and takes off on water. Upon arriving in Iquitos, and enjoying some other adventures we set of on a boat rip on the River Amazon. This was a bigger boat and there were six of us. After the first day's travel we stopped in a settlement and these were different people. A lot of them showed me missing fingers or toes claiming to have been victims of the piranha but during this trip I did not notice any but then again I did not dip a toe in the water. The adventure is worth another book and if I have the energy I shall do it another time.

BBQ IN THE PERUVIAN JUNGLE

STN5 PERU

INSIDE THE MACHU PICHU

TRANS ANDEAN PIPELINE - LOOKING THE PART

# CHINA – THE MIDDLE KINGDOM

Whatever has been written about China is just not enough. It is one of the most ancient civilizations of the world with a vast population and a vast land mass and a complex history. Thus all the people from the beginning of historical records writing about China could not cover all that needs to be said about China.

Here is a country that for most of the 20th century tried to keep all its citizens as Ordinary people but did not succeed. China is now a very powerful nation on the world stage in every aspect and a great Economic power. Historically, it has always been a powerful nation but has always had periods with downward trends and periods of great prosperity. The last such downward period was prolonged and lasted most of the last century.

This chapter is not to narrate the history or geography of China. This is meant to give a different perspective of this Country , its culture , its most attractive landscapes and most important some business tips for people going from the Western world to seek a piece of this large economic pie.

I started travelling to China in the mid to late eighties and although changes had started to take place but one saw a lot of the 'old' China. The bigger cities like Beijing, Guangzhou and Shanghai by then had Western hotels but in the smaller cities not much had changed. In visiting the Factories the Soviet styled Communism influence became clear. The foreign guests or contingents were always received very warmly and the best hospitality was extended .The reception Committee was dominated by the Communist party members who then proceeded to give long speeches highlighting the success and the reasons behind this being the 'best ideology' in the world. Most people dressed in the Mao suits and there was little social chit chat. At meals, every effort was made to shove as much Moutai or similar spirits down the foreigner/s. Moutai has 53% content of alcohol by volume!. Those of us who have survived the many ordeals over 20 years of travelling to China deserve a medal from somewhere. In this particular case it resulted in business worth millions of pounds where the entity was concerned. This is easier said then done.

The Chinese business culture has changed over the last thirty years and the modern businessmen are as smart and stylish as their foreign counterparts. Most of them have been educated overseas and are on top of their game.

In the past it was very much a prolonged ritual to extract a favourable business deal. There was always the strong hand of the State in all organizations and even today most of the successful Chinese multinationals have substantial holdings by the State.

About ten years ago, any text on doing business in China would have been of major interest to people doing or intending to do business in China. However, the modern China is a little more different easier.

In any case some of the ideas below may be of use to the ordinary people going to China:

- Never set unrealistic targets or except things to go smoothly.

- If you are nothing can prepare you for the environment especially outside the larger cities.

- Exercise patience and more patience.

- Most definitely have some Business cards printed with details in Mandarin on the back. Present and accept business cards politely with both hands and take time to look at the cards received so that the other person feels honoured. Business cards are a 'big thing' not only in China but all over South East Asia. Proper protocol always will make an impact. I have seen many a foreign business toss their card to the opposite number and this will forever create the wrong impression. It is offensive to use the left hand to present business cards or documents at any time in Asia.

- Like any other nations, the Chinese appreciate a foreigner being able to speak a few phrases or words of their languages. However, Mandarin the main dialect spoken in mainland China is one of the most difficult language to pronounce. Words with same spelling but different tones may mean very different things. The worst scenario is for a scenario to speak with a terrible pronounciation and embarrass everyone including themselves. Best to stick to English or their own language until  some command of Mandarin is attained

- One can learn a lot about what level of cultural courtesy is required in any one situation by observing the hosts and following some of their actions within a reasonable context. No need to go totally native.

- Do not get into an argument with and officials at the entry or exit points.

- Carry a good stock of your own basic medicine. Having said that medical help is readily available in China and at a very low cost. In fact some of the traditional medicines are really very effective for minor ailments.

- Be ready to face some very exotic and some not so exotic food spreads. This not meant to be derogatory because some of the finest cuisines in the world are Chinese dishes. It is just that there are some unusual offerings which may be hard for the outsiders to swallow – no pun intended. It would be wise to discretely consult the local person assisting the visitor to find out the origins of each dish.

- It is very normal that the host will put on some food using chop sticks on the visitor's plate. It must be accepted graciously accepted and does not need to be eaten if not palatable but some pretence is required. However, the modern Chinese will not go through all that and it is very much straight to the business of eating.

- What has not changed is the complexity of discussions. There will definitely be mind games played and test the patience.

- The Chinese or Asians will not get straight to the point in a business meeting and will start with a general conversation and then move towards the objectives.

- The first meeting will always be conducted in a fairly serious mode but thereafter with familiarity a very relaxed ambience can be the norm if not the rule.

- It is always wise not to discuss local politics or customs. If the hosts decide to comment it is best to listen intently without getting too involved.

- The Chinese and in fact the Asians like to deal with high ranking people with Executive power and they will dig into this very early. If they feel the visitor is not such a high level person and has little or no executive power the meeting will fizzle out.

- It must be the foreign Company strategy to equip their people with some decision making capability and at least give them a 'Title' even though it may be just for this cultural purpose.

- Decision making will be slow and common practise is for the first few meetings to end in a stalemate with signed protocols or Minutes of each meeting.

- Commercial transactions are a lot easier as China has the largest Currency reserves in the world. It was different and very complex some thirty years ago

In general terms the Chinese people have gone through amazing changes in the last forty years. When describing the changes in the lives of people in China no superlative adjective could cover the essence. Major ideological changes have changed the society, the economic and physical well being of the people and their standing in the outside world. Such has been the pace of change that it is actually amazing that apart from the Tinammen Square uprising there has been no other major political upheavels. I guess when people are moving towards prosperity it is easier to accept change.

It is worth while narrating some of the changes that have taken place for the lives of the Chinese people.

As an example in the mid-eighties most of the people you met were just coming out of the aftermath of the Cultural Revolution. What they had endured and gone through is beyond any imagination. People felt left down and almost could not believe that they were headed towards a better life. On some the pain of what they had gone through could be seen on their faces. A lot of them had a limited idea about the outside world. A very distinct feature that was noted that whenever they were invited for a meal they were over excited and then ate with some relish; as if they may not get that opportunity again. In the past the local contacts did not want to socialize much, especially in the evenings. That was a reaction to the past strict controls on the movement of people. I also discovered that those who lived in multi storey state provided apartments had a serious problem as the lift operator's closed shop at 21.00 hrs and thereafter sometimes they had to use the stairs of up to twenty five levels.

Now, that in cities like Beijing and Shanghai where there is an abundance of fine and classy restaurants serving food from around the globe. People are making for the sad past. The trend is to order more than is needed to honour the guest if any and perhaps get the feeling of economic strength. Chinese people now visit the latest chic outlets for food and order as much they can to eat and drink even though it might be Cordon bleu cookery and the most expensive European wines. One way to bury the past.

I have a very good friend who actually is not an ordinary person but an extra ordinary man. From what I understand, his parents were school teachers and were put in a labour camp with the entire family and were forced to work on a farm for long hours and in all weather conditions. Some parts of China are bitterly cold! My friend's mother would wake him up in the late hours and in poor light teach him the English language. My friend responded but his brother did not. As the Cultural Revolution started to come to its end, the government looked for all people with some knowledge of English. My friend was one of the luck one's to be found and he was put on a fast track To a Degree in English and posted abroad as a Commercial officer within the Diplomatic service. Upon his return it did not take him long to move out of the government to become as a consultant and a go between Foreign companies and local entities. He had made many powerful contacts in his time with the Government and many hurdles were removed for him as became one of the very few independent entrepreneur of the that time. I am sure it was not so easy for many others but my friend had a strong character, the self-discipline and a very likeable personality to grab every opportunity that came his way. He is now a millionaire and enjoying life in a way which was beyond his dreams and expectations some forty years ago.

The areas of China in the closer proximity to Hong Kong were always ahead in the development cycle. I guess both HK and China are lucky to have each other. As an example, to do business with China and especially within the Southern part, one had to set up contacts in HK. The deals were done in HK, payments were made there and goods delivered to a local agent. How these got to the other side in spite of hefty tariffs and other barriers? was the secret that brought great prosperity to the this former British Colony and indeed to the Southern part of China. Things were different for the Central, Northern and Eastern parts of China which needed a more traditional approach as narrated earlier.

The changing culinary style of the Chinese has been narrated  and inevitably the foreign cuisines have penetrated the taste buds and palates of the people. However, China has over centuries been well known for many fine cuisines and exotic dishes of its own. Modern "Eight Cuisines" of China are Anhui, Cantonese, Fujian, Hunan, Jiangsu, Shandong, Sichuan, and Zhejiang cuisines. The cuisines are all derived from centuries of gastronomical refinements and some of the dishes are indeed based on herbal medicines. The regional variations are of course due to the vast area of the country and the availability of distinct ingredients such as unique vegetables, seasonings and spices. The variety of dishes in a meal reflect the Chinese traditions and culture and the belief in ying and yang , the qi which is energy and are balance in terms of gastric qualities.

The most popular Chinese cuisine which has transcended borders and cultures is of course the Cantonese ( Guandong ) style of food . It is the most popular style in the South extending to HK who have popularized it all over the world.

The Hunan cuisine is based on a Hot & Sour flavour and is actually the most spicy food from this country. Most people believe that the Sichuan cuisine offers the most spicy option but not so. The Sichuan dishes are spicy and numbing.

There are other regional sub-variations of the cuisines such as the Xinjiang cuisine from the North West influenced by the Muslim culture and based on the Central Asian republics fondness of barbequed meat and bread. The Tibetan Cuisine which is a blend of the Nepalese, Indian and Sichuan flavours.

Apart from all these wonderful and glorious options of feasting. In the coastal regions and especially in the South, there is abundant Sea Food and is very popular especially with the HK residents. The variety of sea food cooked in the different HK style is as good as anywhere else in the world.

Chinese throughout the vast country have become very cosmopolitan and are used to foreigners. In the past they were sometimes quite stunned to see odd liking foreign people. It so happened that I was visiting a small town in the North East of China during summer time. The town is called Qi Qi Har when I say small the current population is 5.3 million but might have been half of that at the time that I am talking about around 1987. It was relatively warm day and I was walking around in short sleeves and with my dark complexion and hairy arms a podgy physique definitely stood out. A bus was going past and suddenly it screeched to a halt. As I looked up I saw the driver had braked as he wanted to have a closer look at me. In the meantime the inquistive passengers had also sensed something odd was on the loose and they were all half hanging out of the windows and some even got off and came for a closer inspection. I got a little worried but when some pretty young ladies decided to touch my hairy arms and inspect my touch I suddenly felt very relaxed.

In the larger cities it was much easier and I stayed with friends in their apartments in very local areas and went to the local shops and the tea shops where the locals get together and play mah jong and cards and spit at will. After the initial intrigue I was no more a novelty. People were always extremely friendly.

Other than that right from when I started to travel the larger cities had very good International hotels and the chains like Sheraton, Hilton, Holiday Inn etc

Had been there for some years. It was when travelling to the not so big cities that the fun started. Almost of all such hotels were state owned so the staff had no training in any aspect of the normal services and perhaps due to lack of motivation there is only one attitude they knew and that was to be rude or indifferent to guests. The rooms were always well heated and that was just as well in places like Harbin, Shenyang which record temperatures of − 25 Deg C in the winter months. The rooms had not so clean bed sheets and quilts and lighting was always dim.  Each hotel had a restaurant which only opened for a few hours a day. If one was accompanied by an influential local person beer would be made available as a special treat. However around 21.00 hrs each night all the power was cut off and you were told firmly by the security guards to go to bed.

Hot water only came on for 15 mins in the morning at 07.00 and for half an hour in the evening. If those slots were missed then it was bad luck for your hosts and the rest.

If one was lucky at breakfast you got a hot cup of tea, the rest of the spread consisted of cold dishes and not one ever looked palatable.

All this changed by the. Frequent stops during journey 90s and with the arrival of hotels like the Shangri La hotels which brought out all that was needed by the foreign business people travelling to China. Within ten years the quality hotels of all grades appeared everywhere. Also with the freeing up of the economy the state owned tourism companies improved their lot and stays in China became a lot easier.

Special mention must be made of the Horizon lounges of the Shangri La hotels not only in China but wherever they have a hotel. These are for the premium guests willing to pay a bit more. That extra amount ensured you were in extra secure areas, there was a lounge with office facilities for up to 16 hours a day. The staff manning these lounges were well trained to offer total assistance to the guests. On top of that food and refreshments are available throughout. Over the last ten years the hotel prices have crept up by alarming levels and hence the Hotels owned by Chinese Companies which are quasi State entities are becoming a good and an acceptable option.

Getting around China has become a lot easier with the massive infra-structure projects having been completed resulting in thousands of kilometres of new highways , new fast train routes using Foreign technology , upgrading of over 50 domestic airports to International standards.

All the development is the best thing for China but somehow the old charm of travelling on a train from North East China to Beijing for thirty hours is gone. One could learn a lot about China by travelling on trains, in the past. A first-hand view of rural China came into view. Even under strict Communist rule the entrepreneurial spirit of the Chinese could not be suppressed. Frequent stops in smaller places brought about a frenzy of activity by different vendors selling a multitude of food and other essential goods. These trains always had a very good dining room meant for the elite of the Chinese society and the foreigners and the offerings were always. The highways are good in China but it is safe to say that the Chinese driving habits are still evolving. The growth of the Automobile population is also astounding. The best estimates point to some 2m Vehicles in 1980 to 154 m vehicles in 2016. China is now a large scale manufacturer, exporter and an importer of all luxury brands.

A mention of the fate of VW Company must be made. In the dark days of the Cultural Revolution, VW virtually gave away their lower end technology of the time to China to the small Chinese Motor manufacturing industry, one factory in Particular base in Shanghai. The result was that when the growth came VW Joint venture benefitted for many years as the no.1 supplier and dominated the market until as such time the needs and trends changed towards other Auto manufacturers.

Today the best way to get around China is by air. There are many domestic airlines all competing with each other and hence much improved service on the ground and in the air is available. The majority of the airports have been built in the last twenty years and have the lounges and all the modern day facilities. This is a far cry from the days when the airports were chaos. Before collecting the Boarding of pass one had to try and buy three different types of tax coupons in a situation where there were no queues. After securing the boarding pass it was another struggle to get past security with officers trying to read the Western name on the boarding pass and comparing it to the name on the Passport. Very few people almost nil spoke English at the airports. There was additional paranoia for flights flying south due to the high incidence of plane hi-jacking to Taiwan. The planes were old Soviet models or domestically assembled rickety things. The planes were dirty. In the pre-computer days there was no seat allocation in fact one was lucky to have their name on the telex sheet with confirmed passenger names. Service was the worst in the world with cardboard boxes with soggy sandwiches and other offerings tossed towards passengers for good measure. One did not have a chance to decline one of these wonderful offerings. The best bet was that someone between you and the air crew got up from their seat and then they got splattered and you escaped from the torture. Thus, it is a great achievement that the Chinese Domestic Airline industry has progressed so much. I would go as far in saying that for the premium market they are better than the domestic air travel in the USA, India and even some parts of Europe.

China has changed in very basic things that touch our lives every day e.g. Pre 1993 the foreigners were not supposed to transact in the local currency, RMB or the people's money. Foreign currency was exchanged for FECs (Foreign Currency Certificates) and these were only acceptable at places where the outsiders were meant to go. Very few Credit Cards were accepted in those days and the verification was slow from the huge logs that they were provided by the Card issuers to check for defaulters. In the present day China there are no issues for foreigners to spend and buy from private traders or multinational shopping malls.

More and more people speak English and other foreign languages in China and that has made the communication much easier when travelling through the country. Not many years ago, I remember once I was dropped at the Beijing Capital Airport for a domestic flight to travel to Shenzen. After struggling through all the hurdles when I arrived at the gate there were no signs of any ground staff and on the Board a lot of words were written in red. Of course I knew there was a problem with the flight. Could I find someone to explain to me as to what the matter was? NO. Must people kept saying No speak English. I could just about state the flight no.in Mandarin and what hour! The answer I got was no hour!!! I struggled back from the gate towards the terminal and the check in area which was next to the International departure Check ins. That was not easy going against the incoming flow of masses and countless Security guards. Finally, I made it but to my shock and horror not one International check in was open and not many people were around that section of the airport. Correspondingly there was hardly anyone around in the arrival area either. There were a couple of disinterested Customs officer lounging around and of course did not speak English! Finally a taxi tout who knew a bit of English helped out for a princely sum of RMB 50 for two minutes interpretation. There was no mystery to the flight with 'no hour status' it was just two hours late. So back through the hazardous course to the departure gate.

The world does not credit Chinese people who are after all the one's responsible for bringing about and absorbing the epoch change. I believe this is so that a great majority of the Chinese are very intelligent human beings they are all natural entrepreneurs and have innovative minds. I cannot understand how Communism and Central Control was ever going to fully work in this country.

There are over 50m Overseas Chinese resulting from historical migration. Majority of them are in the close proximity of the motherland and within Asia but significant numbers can be found in most places on this earth. Wherever they are they will be successful in economic terms and contribute significantly to their new nations. In spite of their above average contribution they are always treated with suspicion even though some of their ancestors migrated more than 150 years ago. They are often subjected to violent treatment defying all laws of morality and civilization.

I believe this above average achievements have something to do with their intelligence levels which are stretched from childhood when they set about trying to learn their language. There many different versions of the language spoken in China but the most common is the Mandarin which is also the official language of the nation. Most dialects are based on symbolic alphabet and as an estimate a child needs to memorize something like 3500 symbols and letters at a very tender age.

There are foreigners who have learnt the Mandarin language properly and thoroughly. I marvel at such people. Most people learn the Pin Yin form an Anglosized version.

I have always managed to learn different languages very quickly but I did struggle with Mandarin and the main reason is that same words with different sound notations have different pronunciations and different meanings. Furthermore, the regional variations of spoken Mandarin are unbelievably different. In some questions the motivation was destroyed when after much practise I tried to speak Mandarin to the Chinese people who either burst out laughing or did not understand me at all and talked back in sign language or worst they replied in English.

Last word on the Chinese language. To a certain extent it is true that there is only one written form of the language and this consists mostly of symbols. Texts written in this form are read with ease by people speaking other dialects and when they read the same text may not be understood by Mandarin speakers as they are not familiar with that dialect. Simply amazing.

*__THE LONELY PLANET ........... SIGHTS WORTH TAKING A LOOK AT__*


-   THEGREAT WALL - BADALING
-   THE FORBIDDEN CITY - BEIJING
-   THE SUMMER PALACE - BEIJING
-   TERRACOTA ARMY – XIAN – EMPREROR QIN'S BURIED BATTALIONS AND
    THE NEWLY DISCOVERED SITES NEARBY
-   GIANT PANDAS IN CHENGDU THEIR NATURAL HABITAT
-   THE BUND IN SHANGHAI
-   THREE GORGES AND THE DAM – CRUISE
-   GUILIN AND THE CRUISE ON RIVER LI
-   THE CLASSICAL GARDENS OF SUZHOU
-   SHILIN STONE FOREST
-   ZHEJIANG: THOUSAND ISLAND LAKE
-   HARBIN ICE LANTERN FESTIVAL

## MALAYSIA ……… THE BEST

I first started travelling to Malaysia in the mid eighties and did not like the place as most of my visits were short and typical business trips. I came over in 1996 and spent a week closely viewing the life style here and have since made this my home.  For me this is my home with a beautiful family and the greatest place to live on this planet.

I consider myself blessed and very privileged to be living in this beautiful country. I am grateful to have peace and serenity in my life and a beautiful Malaysian family and my wonderful wife who is a kind, considerate life partner and my best friend.

Malaysia is a unique country and that is an understatement, it is simply a wonderful place – safe, with many exotic beaches and rain forests, tropical weather, good law and order, multi –cultural, as a result there are a variety of fusion aromatic foods, warm hearted people and just an overall relaxed ambient. For me the most important thing is that the country portrays a very positive and impressive image of Islam. Sceptical people about the religion of Islam are simply amazed when they visit Malaysia. It has to be said that the Muslims in Malaysia are very devout and strict in their practices but let the others follow their own ideals.

Malaysia is a truly multi-cultural nation and there is nowhere else like it. Naturally, any mix of different races can never be perfect and there are bound to be some misunderstandings and a certain amount of negative feelings. Malaysia contains all this as well. It is everyone's hope and prayer that long may peace and serenity last and the extremists on every side are defeated in their evil agenda to keep Malaysia as the wonderful place that it is today.

Malaysian leaders have worked hard to eliminate abject poverty and that is one of the reasons the population remains calm and reasonably satisfied. Malaysia is marching on towards attaining the status of a fully developed country and it is almost there. Rich in resources e.g. Oil & Gas, Palm Oil, Rubber etc it has also built up a very advanced and strong Manufacturing industry and for its relatively small size it is one of the leading exporters of commodities and goods on a global stage.

Most of the progress has been achieved by placing a strong emphasis on education and until now two shifts of schools are run in urban and rural areas to ensure that the country achieves its target of 100% literacy. More or less this has been achieved. One of the largest Government budget allocation is for Education and its development. Malaysians place a great emphasis on education for the future generations and this must contribute to the social order that exists in the country as well as the economic progress that is taking place.

Malaysian population is roughly around 30 Million. Of this some 20 million are the indigenous Malays who are pre-dominantly Muslims. Malays are normally very gentle and polite people and I happen to be married to a very nice Malay lady. She retains her gentleness most of the time but every now and then she becomes quite like the rest of us. She says that this is due to the extreme provocation by her partner? There are about 6 Million descendants of the Chinese people who migrated to this part of the world more than 150 years ago. They came here and inevitably set up the Trading infrastructure and as a result the current generation are the most prosperous community. There are about 2 million descendants of the Indian people who came here over a hundred years ago under the British rule for a variety of jobs on plantations, the police, the Army etc the balance of the population is the different ethnic tribes especially from Eastern Malaysia.

Malaysia consists of thirteen states and three federal territories and has a total landmass of 330,803 square kilometres (127,720 sq mi) separated by the South China Sea into two similarly sized regions, Peninsular Malaysia and East Malaysia (previously North Borneo) now the states of Sarawak, Sabah and the Federal territory of Labuan.

Of the 11 states in Peninsular Malaysia, nine have traditional rulers who have a role to play in Modern Malaysia. These nine rulers amongst themselves elect the King of Malaysia every five years and this rotation process ensures that this honour is shared. The king of Malaysia then appoints Governors of the state without monarchy in consultation with the ruling Chief Minister of the relevant State Government.

The executive power is with the federal Government duly elected by the people of Malaysia, who also elect the state legislature.

FOOD

Malaysian food is simply wonderful, the variety, the fusion, the spices, the aroma are simply amazing. Malaysians also love their food and are totally spoiled for choice and eating is a national pastime. Further evidence of this food being nutritious and healthy is that there is very little obesity amongst the people. People in Malaysia seem to eat from the crack of dawn till the early hours and accordingly food is available at all hours.

In my unofficial estimate that for a population of 30m there most be close to 5m eateries in Malaysia.

Malaysian cuisine consists of cooking traditions and practices found in Malaysia, and reflects the multi ethnic makeup of its population.

As a result of historical migrations, colonisation by foreign powers, and its geographical position within its wider home region, Malaysia's culinary style in the present day is primarily a melange of traditions from its Malay, Chinese, Indian, Indonesian and ethnic Bornean citizens, with heavy to light influences from Thai, Portuguese, Dutch, and British cuisines, to name a few. This resulted in a symphony of flavours, making Malaysian cuisine highly complex and diverse.

Because Peninsular Malaysia shares a common history with Singapore, it is common to find versions of the same dishes across both sides of the border regardless of place of origin, such as laksa and chicken rice. Also because of their proximity, historic migrations and close ethnic and cultural kinship, Malaysia shares culinary ties with Indonesia, as both nations often share certain dishes, such as satay, rendang and sambal.

Malaysia also has some of the finest tropical fruits in abundance including the awful smelling Durian which is loved by most Asians and they refer to it as the King of all fruits.

I personally prefer Bananas, Pineapple, Papaya, Water Melon, mango steen etc

Thus, it is a matter of no surprise that most Malaysians do not want to leave their country and do become home sick very quickly if they do have to spend time away.

LONELY PLANET

One has to start with Kuala Lumpur a great metropolis with a lot to offer. A really happening place and one of the best cities of Asia as it is not over burgeoning like many other places in this continent.

KL as it is popularly known has its origins from the 1840s but now is very much modern city with an impressive skyline featuring some of the tallest structures in the world. KL is also known for some of the most impressive shopping malls in the world. It has something for everyone and is a relatively safe place to relax and enjoy quality time.

All the leading chains of hotels are present in Malaysia and the service for the better part is beyond expectations. Some of the hotels offer the old Colonial charms

There are many wonderful places to visit in Malaysia, from a personal experience point of view, I shall highlight the following;

- Langkawi at any of the following hotels Datai bay , Tanjung Rhu and the Four Seasons

*FOUR SEASONS*

THE DATAI

TANJONG RHU BEACH

_PENANG – AT SHANGRI LA RASA SAYANG_

_PANGKOR LAUT – ONE HOTEL, ONE ISLAND_

*CAMEROON HIGHLANDS*

*SHANGRI LA RASA RIA, SABAH*

TIOMAN ISLAND

REDANG ISLAND/TERRENGANU – IN SEASON TO SEE THE LARGE TURTLES

# SOUTH KOREA

There are no other countries in the world that have such a heavily militarized border as do South and North Korea. The historical split of the two countries is as a result of the conflict of Super powers with different ideologies influencing the nations. Japan had occupied the country since 1910 and had ravaged the nation beyond belief. After the end of the second world war in 1945, Russia and the USA were both responsible for the division of the country based on their ideologies. Russia supported Kim Il-Sung and they were backed by China. US supported South Korean leaders claiming to be the forbearers of Democracy. A tragic and a bloody civil war followed from 1950 – 53 where each side supported by their larger allies had pushed each other  to the edge but finally there as  a result of a stalemate in the military successes and with UN intervention, there was relief for both sides. The 1953 armistice, never signed by South Korea, split the peninsula along the demilitarized zone near the original demarcation line. No peace treaty was ever signed, resulting in the two countries remaining technically at war. The two countries remain hostile towards each other and the main border posts at Paju Kun have become tourist attractions. There is nothing amusing about two nuclear armed nations blaring out propaganda at each other across this symbolic line. From the South Korean side the North looks pretty grim with people working on farms with manual gadgets in run down shacks. If there was ever a stark contrast to be observed between the two ideologies this border by default must be the best portrayal.

South Korea land base is 70% mountainous hence the agriculture is limited and the country is reliant on imports large quantities of fruit and vegetables. Otherwise some of the landscape is very beautiful with mountains and a beautiful coast and islands.

There are a lot of Palaces Buddhist temples and ancient cities to highlight the great dynasties and Empires of the past. The culture of the Koreans is neither Japanese or Chinese but their history has been intertwined with the other two. They share the same alphabet but their language known as the Hangeul is very original and they are very proud of it.

Known as the Land of the morning calm which in translation has a meaning closer to K O R E A. It is also called the 'Hermit Kingdom' where for long periods of its history it tried to close itself from outside influences to avoid wars and being occupied. From the end of the Civil war to about the late eighties it tried to keep a low profile as it built itself into a powerful Industrial nation right at the forefront of Technology.

I first had the privilege of visiting this country in the late 80s and it was a very interesting experience to be in a 'hermit' state. The Koreans were mostly used to the Americans as the foreigners and were not exposed to Asian looking people like myself, so I was a rarity and a subject of intrigue. Very few Koreans at that time were allowed to travel abroad. The one's that did were mostly the Government staff or high level private sector businessmen. Very few people understood or spoke good English, not that this a judgement but was a practical difficulty at that time. South Korea was a prosperous nation then due to the sheer hard work by its people all of whom seemed to work six days a week. They were in the midst of hosting the 1988 Olympics which was the first glimpse the world caught of this country and everyone was impressed

After the end of the Civil War for a long period the country was under the rule of Military dictators, perhaps that was needed to bring stability to the country and safeguard its security as the North Koreans were always at clandestine games to cause maximum damage to their brethren in the South. Gen Park ruled the country from 1960 till his assassination in 1979. He was a ruthless military dictator but he laid the foundations of modern Korea. In the 70s the large business groups in collusion with the Government led the way with a rapid export led growth, world class infrastructure was developed, sound education policies were implemented and Korea became one of the so called Asian Economic Tigers. The large Industrial groups Samsung, Hyundai, Lucky Gold Star, Daewoo and a host of others became household names and their areas of business were vast. The Japanese model of the government and the Business (especially these large groups called the Chaebol) working together gave South Korea a very dynamic growth for a few years. Thousands of Koreans workers who had gone to earn a higher wage in the Middle East returned home to the many new opportunities at home.

However, dictatorships and large Industrial concerns created periods of political and Industrial instability and further pressure from the army rulers did not satisfy the people. As the world economies slowed down in 1990 and then 1997, South Korea suffered some of its worst economic times during the 1997 Asian Economic crisis as it re-structured its economy from significant reliance on the Heavy Industries to a better mix of traditional areas with the High end technology.

Modern Korea has arrived, companies like Samsung are challenging Sony for the technological leadership. The seeds of the Education system laid many decades have given the best Human capital and the top R & D to the local landscape.

In social terms South Koreans are some of the most avid travellers around the world and in reverse over 10 million global tourists visit what was or still is the 'Hermit Kingdom'. The social scene has changed beyond belief and the younger generation are as forward moving as any other nation. South Korea' art scene has gained popularity and many of the local Movies and TV soap Operas have fanatical following worldwide. It is a little bit of a surprise that a nation gained influence around the world through its arts i.e. movies and TV programmes to the extent that it influenced the purchasing habits of consumers in International markets.

South Korea is now the 11$^{th}$ largest economy of the world and one of the highest per capita incomes on a PPP basis.

Sadly, the only thing that is not on the right track is the relationship with the neighbours North Korea. In fact the current situation is very serious as Nuclear weapons are being flaunted by the North gaining the ire of the USA and President Trump. A likely war scenario is not even worth imagining as the Capital City Seoul virtually stands on the border and well within the range of Conventional guns let alone nuclear war heads. In such a sad scenario Japan is also very vulnerable and parts of China are in the immediate range. One can only hope for good sense to prevail and peaceful means to be found to settle the dispute.

South Korea co-hosted the Soccer World Cop with Japan in 2002 and it was one of the most successful Global event of its kind ever held. The organizational capabilities of the South Koreans were evident during the month long event and I was privileged to be there in Seoul for part of the tournament. It was like being at a well-organized party with a great ambience. Everyone joined hands to enjoy and laugh and witness great games of Soccer.

As it was, the South Korean Soccer team performed beyond expectations so that ramped up the fervour of the people. There was not the minutest acrimony or anger. People danced in the streets after games and at the end of the day the South Koreans got together and helped collect the rubbish and clean up the streets. It was a spectacle like never before and I have never experienced anything so memorable.

In terms of people, Koreans are wonderful and kind people. My best friend and in fact I call him my younger brother has been a real friend for thirty years. When circumstances took me to a bachelor status for the second time in my life he travelled from Seoul to be with me for each of my birthdays. There are so many tales of his kindness.

In terms of visiting South Korea and disregarding all the tensions, Seoul is on of the grandest cities in the world. Like most great cities it is separated by a large river in this case the River Han.

 The Seoul Capital Area contains five UNESCO World Heritage Sites: Changdeok Palace, Hwaseong Fortress, Jongmyo Shrine, Namhansanseong and the Royal Tombs of the Joseon Dynasty. Seoul is surrounded by mountains, the tallest being Mt. Bukhan, the world's most visited national park per square foot.Modern landmarks include the iconic N Seoul Tower, the gold-clad 63 Building, the  Dongdaemun Design Plaza, Lotte World, the world's largest indoor theme park, Moonlight Rainbow Fountain, the world's longest bridge fountain and the Sevit Floating Islands. The birthplace of K-pop and the Korean. The largest wholesale and retail market in South Korea, the Dongdaemun Market, is located in Seoul. Myeongdong is a shopping and entertainment area in downtown Seoul with mid- to high-end stores, fashion boutiques and international brand outlets.The nearby Namdaemun Market, named after the Namdaemun Gate, is the oldest continually running market in Seoul.


Insadong is the cultural art market of Seoul, where traditional and modern Korean artworks, such as paintings, sculptures and calligraphy are sold.Hwanghak-dong Flea Market and Janganpyeong Antique Market also offer antique products. Some shops for local designers have opened in Samcheong-dong, where numerous small art galleries are located. In the past Itaewon had catered mainly to foreign tourists and American soldiers based in the city, Koreans now comprise the majority of visitors to the area.

Seoul has something for everyone and is a kind of a 'happening' place.

No visit to this country is complete without a tour of the demilitarized zone. In spite of the tension there are many tourist areas including observatories from where one can glance across to the other side, a peace park, the most northern Dorasan station from where the barbed wires separating the two countries can be seen. Over the years four tunnels were discovered, these were dug up by the North Koreans to surprise the South and some of these could allow a large number of troops to move through and cross the border unnoticed.

Whilst there is a lot of variety of night time entertainment available all over South Korea. One of the most outstanding art form is the Fan Dance. Years ago there used to be a daily performance at the Sheraton Hill Walker Hotel and that was simply breath taking.

A reasonable driving distance from Seoul are the Andong Hahoe Village and Gyeongju Yangdong Village are historical villages that were developed during the 14th to 15th century in Gyeongsangbuk-do. These two villages are well-preserved examples of typical Korean clan villages based on descents whose members carry the same family name derived from common ancestors. Even today, these families live in the village and continue their meaningful legacy, making the whole village a living and active cultural heritage.

A fast train from Seoul city centre can take you to Gwangju or Busan. From Gwangju the historic sites are accessible e.g. Gyeongju by bus or other means.

Busan is the second largest city in South Korea and with its large beach area is very popular with the local tourists.

Gyeongju Historic Area is a historical attraction where the achievements and culture of the Silla Dynasty (57BC – AD 935) have remained well-preserved. In the Gyeongju area, capital city of Silla, there are many sites and monuments important to the 1,000 years of development of Korean architecture and Buddhism. The area is divided into 5 zones based on their characteristics: the Namsan Mountain area, a center of Buddhist culture; the Wolseong Fortress area, the royal grounds of the Silla Dynasty; the Daereungwon Tomb area, the tombs of high-ranking officials including the kings of the Silla Dynasty; the Hwangnyongsa Temple area, showing the essence of Silla Buddhism; and the Sanseong Fortress area, focusing on the defensive mechanisms of the royal capital.

Korean cuisine is largely based on rice, noodles, tofu, vegetables, fish and meats. Traditional Korean meals are noted for the number of side dishes, banchan, which accompany steam-cooked short-grain rice. Every meal is accompanied by numerous banchan. Kimchi, a fermented, usually spicy vegetable dish is commonly served at every meal and is one of the best known Korean dishes. Korean cuisine usually involves heavy seasoning with sesame oil, doenjang , a type of fermented soybean paste, soy sauce, salt, garlic, ginger, and gochujang , a hot pepper paste. Other well-known dishes are Bulgogi , grilled marinated beef, Gimbap , and Tteokbokki , a spicy snack consisting of rice cake seasoned with gochujang or a spicy chili paste.

Soups are also a common part of a Korean meal and are served as part of the main course rather than at the beginning or the end of the meal. Soups known as guk are often made with meats, shellfish and vegetables.

Popular Korean alcoholic beverages include Soju, Makgeolli and Bokbunja ju. Of which Soju is a personal favourite. It can be up to 53 % alcohol by volume. Traditionally, it was made from Rice, wheat and barley. Modern versions rely on other starches.

The best way to enjoy an evening in Seoul is to have good Bulgogi accompanied by Soju and the background traditional music. Spending a bit of time in South Korea can be infectious as the very deep and profound culture takes over and one can start to loose one's self.

# THE WONDERS OF AIR TRAVEL

… those magnificent men and their flying machines (Anon)

In the span of some 60 odd years the changes related to Air travel are prodigious and not even the Major airlines could have predicted the phenomenon and that is perhaps why a great many of these brand names are now no more e.g. BOAC , BEA , PAN AM AND TWA . It is fascinating to see that a leading airline from sixty years ago holds its own in the current times and that is KLM − The Royal Dutch Airlines. A short synopsis of reasons for their longevity will be discussed.

All air travel in the past was equivalent to the business class/first class travel of current times. The Economy Class legroom was larger than the space offered in First Class of Today. I do not know why people bothered to pay for First class travel in those days. As very few people travelled there were no issues at check ins. Every passenger was more or less a VIP. If the passenger had to transit en route. The airline took care of everything inclusive of meals, transfers and the best hotels. Of course the air travel was expensive in terms of the spending power of the consumers at that time.

Readers may be wondering where this is leading too. I have been travelling International routes by air for around 60 years and am a self-appointed critic of the Airlines. If this publication is accepted my next ambition is to take on the role of a full time critic and writer on experiences with different Airlines. It is something we all would like to do because we do not have Private Jets or VIP status and often suffer indignities that as paying customers we should not have to endure.

So why take the long route and why not get to the point? I believe it is worth spending a bit of time to get an historical perspective on the subject.

In my opinion an airline should be judged on the following parameters:

Safety record

Value for money

Reliability

On ground services

Onboard appearance – cleanniness, livery etc

Service On Board

Food – Beverages

In appendix one is an analysis of all these parameters for some of the so called leading airlines of today.

We can start by looking at the longest surviving airlines.

KLM Royal Dutch Airlines, It is part of the Air France–KLM group, and is a member of the SkyTeam airline alliance. KLM was founded in 1919; it is the oldest airline in the world still operating under its original name.

KLM have always had a professional level of Service which they have maintained for a very long time. This service is not the best but always professional. They also have the advantage of one of the best connected airports in Europe, Schipol. Although now ageing but I believe it has helped KLM's longevity. In a lighter vein the charming Dutch stewardesses who are very courteous and very tall are most definitely terrorist deterrents!

## QANTAS

Holds title of the "Second oldest operating Airline by Years in service", after KLM. As well as the "Oldest Continuously Operating Airline in the World." Due to KLM suspending service during WW2.

This airline has to be recognized for its longevity and quite a good safety record. In terms of service it is quite reasonable. The Aussie friendly and somewhat informal style prevails. This works for me but maybe not for everyone.

## AIR FRANCE

Air France, stylized as AIRFRANCE, is the French flag carrier headquartered in Tremblay-en-France, (north of Paris). It is a subsidiary of the Air France–KLM Group and a founding member of the SkyTeam global airline alliance. The predecessor of Air France was founded on the same day as KLM on the 7th October 1919. A series of mergers takes the original identity away.

Frankly, I cannot understand why they have survived so long, must be due to the alliances and routes which other airlines do not fly to.

The air crew are well trained and very courteous and defy the normal unfriendly character of the French.

## FINNAIR

Finnair is the fifth oldest airline in the world with uninterrupted existence. With no fatal or hull-loss accidents since 1963, Finnair is consistently on the list of safest airlines in the world (#3 in 2014).Founded   1 November 1923

Perhaps a less well known airline but very successful on the routes that it serves. In the days before the breakup of the Soviet Union this airline was the best option to travel between Europe and Bejing, China. Their food was always very delectable and the variety of the selection of wines always pleasing.

LUFTHANSA

Two years after the Allies dissolved the first Lufthansa (founded in 1926) in 195_, the "Aktiengesellschaft für Luftverkehrsbedarf" (Luftag) with headquarters in Cologne was founded on January 6, 1953.  On August 6, 1954 Luftag bought the name, the trademark – the crane – and the colors – blue and yellow – from the first Lufthansa, which was in liquidation at the time, and has since then called itself "Deutsche Lufthansa Aktiengesellschaft" (Deutsche Lufthansa Stock Company). Multiple tasks had to be accomplished by the new airline before  t could begin flight traffic: finding and buying suitable airplanes, schooling airline pilots and engineers and training air stewards. Organizational and infrastructural prerequisites for the technical maintenance of airplanes also had to be set. The ambitious project succeeded: on April 1, 1955 two Convair airplanes took off from Hamburg and Munich to commence scheduled air services.

In 1960, Lufthansa arrived in the age of the jet plane with the acquisition of the first Boeing B707. Simultaneously, the company transferred its long-distance operations from Hamburg to Frankfurt Main and continued to expand its cargo business.

The only reason this airline is mentioned because it was the first airline that I travelled on and obviously the first experience of being air borne which is always cherished in the memory. It is akin to loosing one's air travel virginity! I remember it was a Boeing 707 and most of the co-travellers were European. The air crew were all tall blond and beautiful German ladies. So my mother an Asian lady with four children from the age range of 10 to 1 year old were different type of passengers for that flight. Let it be known that for that time in the sub-continent, unusually my mother was a qualified Medical Doctor and a confident English speaker. There was just the lack of experience in terms of International travel.

I was most excited as I was seating a row away from the rest of the family and felt very important when assisted by the flight crew to fasten my seat belt. I had a fair knowledge of English and had met many foreigners and knew that the accents of the British were different to the Amercians. However, listening to the German speakers confused me. **It suddenly dawned on me that not all white people**

**spoke English.** We take off in the middle of the night and I soon fell asleep. Upon waking a few hours later in transit at Beriut airport, I suddenly realized we were the only people on board the aircraft as everyone else had gone to the Transit lounge. I created mini-panic for my mother by hysterically claiming that we had arrived at our destination and we needed to get off or would end up somewhere else. I was calmed down by one of the ground staff. As I calmed down I decided to occupy the window seat in my row and luckily the passenger who was the rightful occupant did not mind and just smiled at me upon his return back to the aircraft. Back in the air dawn was breaking and I could see we were above the clouds which confused me as I always thought above the clouds was very close to heaven. Suddenly, I noticed that the plane had no propellers. I had only known and seen aero planes with propellers until then. So I started exclaiming that we were going to crash as the plane had lost its propellors . Luckily, other than my own family no one else understood my message of Doom.

A mention of the so called the world's favourite airline must be introduced at this point.

BRITISH AIRWAYS

I am very proud to be British. I love all things about Great Britain. I support the England Cricket team against every other nation, I am almost fanatical about the English Soccer team and I am always cheering for England when it comes to Rugby Union. In spite of the fact I that have lived away from England for the last twenty years, I still listen to Sky News every morning and keep in touch. I am a Royalist and have had the privilege to bow to Her Majesty and shake her hand during her visit to KL, Malaysia for the 1998 Commonwealth games.

I pledged over 27 years ago that I would never travel BA ever again as a result of the appalling attitude of an air crew member board a flight. That was not the first time either but that type of arrogant and indifferent attitude was far too regular.

Being a patriot I always preferred to travel with BA. Most of the time the flights were good, service was good and had some good times flying the flag. However.

there is always the odd crew member who have the condescending attitude based on some misguided values and that spoils the whole mix.

Going back to the main topic of air travel, the whole scenario changed once the mass travel became a norm. People started to take more holidays abroad, economic migration snowballed the need to travel. Packaged holidays and cut throat competition enhanced the growth of Charter flights. As a result the airlines maximized the passenger per flight in face of the rising costs of Oil. There were some early pioneers in introducing the low cost air travel but none had any great success. The model was mostly applied to within the USA and Trans-Atlantic routes. Laker was one name that dominated this markets sector for a while but then collapsed. One of the great entrepreneurs of our time, Richard Branson came along with Virgin airlines and had his own concept and models for the airline business. He had some falls but always had the ability to make a name for himself.

With arrival of the B747 – the Jumbo jet, it was possible to transport numerically heavier loads to longer distances. Further improvements on fuel consumption enabled flight upward of 14 hours. The development of IT and other related technology facilitated this compound growth in numbers using air travel.

In the early 80s emerged a new standard of Airline travel featuring the upcoming airlines like Singapore Airline, Cathay Pacific, Malaysia Airlines, Thai Air, Japan Airlines (re-invented) , Nippon airlines and South Korean Asiana airlines. They brought a different meaning to service. Perhaps the local cultures played a major role but the type of service on offer could not be matched by the European or US airlines. The concept of being pampered while travelling was alien to most travellers of the time but it was something one could get used to very quickly.

These airlines still are very successful and maintain their positions in the market and continuously improve each aspect of their total service. There are always tie-ups and mergers as in the recent case of Cathay Pacific and Dragon Air.

Coming on the heels of the above from within the region are China Airlines (Taiwan) which has emerged from a disastrous history. Eva Air is also a very good airline dominant on its routes within Asia Pacific. A re-vamped Garuda Airlines is competing well in the region and truly have gone through a complete cultural change and the day is not far away that they will be talked about in the same terms as some of the other carriers from their neighbor hood.

Time and again the industry was hit by rising Oil prices which impacted upon the travel costs and a correspond impact on the fortunes of the Airlines. Other events like regional wars and 9/11 had a terrible impact on the whole sector and even some of the above names had to re-invent themselves.

As always happens this period was used by some of the emerging airlines of the Middle East to take Air travel to another level. These airlines were backed by cash rich countries and relied on brand new aircrafts and some of them were the leading buyers of the A-380 when it was launched.

Emirates, Eithad, Qatar Airways lead the way followed by other smaller lines and have brought about levels of service and luxury to new heights. I have not had the privilege as yet to travel by the first class Apartments on Emirates and Eithad but this is going back to the days of Imperial Airways.

I feel just blessed to be on Business Class on any one of these airlines and many a wonderful journey has gone by with me propping the bar for the bulk of the journey.

Emirates has ever expanding network and the pace they are moving at and not withstanding any catastrophic events they will dominate air travel for some time to come.

Gulf Air also ran for similar honours until it went in a financial tailspin for many different reasons. Oman Air can have a better reputation once the Muscat airport expansion is completed

Another airline that does get mentioned in the same breath as the above is Turkish Airlines. I have to say that in spite of some very plus points they are not on par and the reasons for this become clear in the relevant analysis in the Appendix

Two other airlines must be mentioned for the longevity of their names i.e Swiss Air and Alitalia. The names live on but the financial history has taken away their original identity. In the case of the former this is a surprise because it used to be referred to as the 'flying bank'. SwissAir is now owned by Lufthansa and after much turmoil Alitalia is now 49% owned by Eithad.

A mention has to be made of Low Cost carriers and there are many around the globe. I will mention only a few, Ryan Air, Easy Jet and Air Asia. The success of Ryan Air is amazing and there model is based on ruthless attitude to give outstanding efficiency. Easy Jet has a good model and is a moderate low cost carrier. However, the best in the world is the Malaysian Air Asia. It has taken the best of the ideas from the established low cost carriers and added the Asian humility and spice to create a unique airline. It starts with their red dressed air stewardesses bound to impress every male passenger for a start. They are as polite as crew from any other premium airline. Their network and alliances are making them hard to beat and simply the value for money that they offer and the best has yet to come.

If there were to be raspberry awards, I would have no hesitation in mentioning the following airlines:

PIA, Aeroflot, Libya Air, Egypt Air, United, American Airlines etc etc

Most of the narration on this subject has been in a positive vein. However, there is the more distressing side to put down on paper and that is the accidents involving air travel. Thankfully, these are rare events but whenever these occur there is always shock and despair.

On 8th March 2104 a Malaysia airlines Flt No.370 flying from KL to Beijing disappeared in a shroud of controversy and till to date there is no explanation. Sadly, it is most likely the reality of this tragedy may never be known. Naturally, the suffering of the bereaved families across borders was stark and poignant. The worst part was that so many theories abounded giving false hope and that is simply painful.

My family and I have been through such a painful experience. On 25th August 1989 a PIA F-27 took of from Gilgit in NW Pakistan bound for the Islamabad airport. A flight of some 55 mins through the most difficult terrain of some of the highest peaks in the world. On board were 54 people including the crew. This included my younger sister, her husband, two sons aged 11 and 4 and a daughter of less than two years. One other son aged 9 at the time had flown out a few days earlier with my parents. The flight just disappeared and no trace has been found until to date. It was not the first accident of this kind on this route but previously pieces of wreckage or some evidence of the crash had been found.

My parents were leading a blissful retirement until that day and that incident just shook their lives. My brother had to fly in from Canada, my sister and family in from London. I heard the news in transit at the Chep Lok Airport, HK flying back from Seoul to London. When I heard the news the shock that went through me was like a severe body blow. There were thousands of people screaming and running around the chaotic airport but no one was listening to me or even looking at this stunned figure. Of course at that time mobile phones were not around. I gathered myself and went to the washroom and sprayed cold water over my face and then just thought for a moment what to do. By then they were calling my name to get on the flight bound for London. Somehow I struggled to the gate and the ground crew realized there was something wrong and assisted me in boarding. How I spent the next 14 hours on the flight, I will never know but I did. Proves a point that humans can endure a lot more than they imagine.

The days that followed were full of speculation with appalling rumours being spread that the aircraft and the passengers were fine but it had been hijacked to Afghanistan by the freedom fighters. Some other stories being spread were that the plane had wandered across the Indian air space and had been shot down. Other absurd tales that it had landed in an unknown valley but people were all safe. The truth probably was that it had crashed into a mountain and got buried in deep snow. No one knows till to date what really happened.

All I know that my mother did not survive this tragedy for too long, she only hung on to care for the nephew who survived by not being on that ill-fated plane. My father was more resolute but in the end it broke him. We could not look at our nephew, a nine year old who had enough sense to grasp this tragedy and the massive loss of his family. Fortunately, the young boy is made of something special because he never cried or discussed the matter. We just did not know what to say to him except tell him that he had all our love.

The suffering of my parents was prolonged for up to three years after that event with stories of sightings of survivors in Afghanistan etc

At that time CNN did not have the coverage as it does now and so this tragedy did not get the coverage it deserved. Most nations of the world assisted with satellite imagery but nothing was ever found.

I did not smile for two years but I had to fight on for the sake of my two young children and also to be in a position to help the nephew. The only positive outcome was that he grew up to be a fine citizen of the world and is happily married with a son of his own.

# AIRLINE: EMIRATES

## GRADING OUT OF TEN. BUSINESS CLASS. ECONOMY CLASS IN RED

| | TYPE OF SERVICE | GRADE | COMMENTS |
|---|---|---|---|
| | BOOKING/RESERVATION | 7  6 | |
| | CHECK IN/ONLINE | 6  5 | NOT GOOD AT KL AND LHR |
| | BASE AIRPORT | 8  8 | |
| | LOUNGE AT BASE AIRPORT | 7  N/A | TOO CROWDED |
| | TRANSIT FACILITIES E.G. SECURITY CLEARANCE ETC | 8  6 | |
| | WELCOME ON BOARD | 7  4 | INCONSISTENT/RUDE GROUND STAFF |
| | SEAT COMFORT | 8  6 | |
| | AMENITIES | 8  5 | |
| | CHOICE OF DRINKS | 8  5 | |
| | FOOD PRESENTATION | 7  4 | |
| | FOOD VARIETY AND QUALITY | 7  5 | |
| | ATTITUDE OF STAFF | 8  6 | |
| | QUALITY OF STAFF | 7  5 | |
| | FACILITIES ON BOARD | 7  6 | |
| | PUNCTUALITY | 9  9 | |
| | DEALING WITH DELAYS | 8  7 | |
| | **TOTAL** | **120**  87 | |

Although as a matter of personal choice, Emirates remain my favourite but sadly they do not emerge as no.1 in the analysis. This is largely because the service is inconsistent and sometimes the food served is poor.

Perhaps, the very thing that they are proud of in terms of having a crew of many different nationalities on board each flight becomes their Achilles heel due to the variation in values and attitudes. Maybe, the management of Emirates need to look at this aspect.

On a brighter note, I have a positive experience to narrate on board Emirates flight no. EK012 from LGW to Dubai. I had Seat no.14E allocated to me in the Business Class section and my Wife had the Seat no.14F. Almost upon boarding I realized the crew members assigned to my side of the aisle were absolutely useless, had no manners or courtesy (probably trainees). Immediately, I brought this matter to the attention of the Cabin Manager Ms Vithya. She listened intently and assured me that I would have a great flight and she would take care of the problem. I did have a great flight as for the rest of the duration My wife and I were served and taken care of by two of the most charming and courteous crew members a Miss Katie from Canada and Miss Zama from South Africa. Every time we needed something they were there. The other two carried on their work for the rest of the passengers but never came near us. This suited us fine. Hats of to Ms .Vithya on how she managed this high altitude manoeuvre. More of this type of crew management and I shall choose Emirates for every possible journey.

**AIRLINE: EITHAD**

**GRADING OUT OF TEN. BUSINESS CLASS.** ECONOMY CLASS IN RED

| | TYPE OF SERVICE | GRADE | COMMENTS |
|---|---|---|---|
| | BOOKING/RESERVATION | 7   7 | |
| | CHECK IN/ONLINE | 6   5 | |
| | BASE AIRPORT | 6   6 | |
| | LOUNGE AT BASE AIRPORT | 8   N/A | |
| | TRANSIT FACILITIES E.G. SECURITY CLEARANCE ETC | 8   6 | |
| | WELCOME ON BOARD | 8   6 | |
| | SEAT COMFORT | 8   5 | |
| | AMENITIES | 8   5 | |
| | CHOICE OF DRINKS | 8   5 | |
| | FOOD PRESENTATION | 8   4 | |
| | FOOD VARIETY AND QUALITY | 9   6 | |
| | ATTITUDE OF STAFF | 8   7 | |
| | QUALITY OF STAFF | 7   5 | |
| | FACILITIES ON BOARD | 6   6 | |
| | PUNCTUALITY | 8   8 | |
| | DEALING WITH DELAYS | 8   7 | |
| | **TOTAL** | **121**   88 | |

## AIRLINE: OMAN AIR

## GRADING OUT OF TEN. BUSINESS CLASS. ECONOMY CLASS IN RED

|  | TYPE OF SERVICE | GRADE | COMMENTS |
|---|---|---|---|
|  | BOOKING/RESERVATION | 7   7 |  |
|  | CHECK IN/ONLINE | 6   5 |  |
|  | BASE AIRPORT | 6   6 |  |
|  | LOUNGE AT BASE AIRPORT | 7   N/A |  |
|  | TRANSIT FACILITIES E.G. SECURITY CLEARANCE ETC | 4   4 |  |
|  | WELCOME ON BOARD | 8   8 |  |
|  | SEAT COMFORT | 9   5 |  |
|  | AMENITIES | 7   5 |  |
|  | CHOICE OF DRINKS | 6   5 |  |
|  | FOOD PRESENTATION | 8   4 |  |
|  | FOOD VARIETY AND QUALITY | 7   5 |  |
|  | ATTITUDE OF STAFF | 8   7 |  |
|  | QUALITY OF STAFF | 7   5 |  |
|  | FACILITIES ON BOARD | 5   5 |  |
|  | PUNCTUALITY | 7   7 |  |
|  | DEALING WITH DELAYS | 8   7 |  |
|  | **TOTAL** | **110   85** |  |

# AIRLINE: TURKISH

## GRADING OUT OF TEN. BUSINESS CLASS. ECONOMY CLASS IN RED

|  | TYPE OF SERVICE | GRADE | | COMMENTS |
|---|---|---|---|---|
|  | BOOKING/RESERVATION | 7 | 7 |  |
|  | CHECK IN/ONLINE | 4 | 4 | TERRIBLE AT EUROPEAN AIRPORTS |
|  | BASE AIRPORT | 6 | 6 |  |
|  | LOUNGE AT BASE AIRPORT | 9 | N/A | CROWDED BUT EXCELLENT |
|  | TRANSIT FACILITIES E.G. SECURITY CLEARANCE ETC. | 7 | 3 |  |
|  | WELCOME ON BOARD | 6 | 4 |  |
|  | SEAT COMFORT | 6 | 6 |  |
|  | AMENITIES | 8 | 5 |  |
|  | CHOICE OF DRINKS | 8 | 5 |  |
|  | FOOD PRESENTATION | 8 | 4 |  |
|  | FOOD VARIETY AND QUALITY | 9 | 5 |  |
|  | ATTITUDE OF STAFF | 6 | 5 | THE ATTITUDE OF FEMALE STAFF IS |
|  | QUALITY OF STAFF | 7 | 5 | EXCELLENT BUT THE MALE STAFF |
|  | FACILITIES ON BOARD | 7 | 6 | TEND TO BE RUDE |
|  | PUNCTUALITY | 7 | 7 |  |
|  | DEALING WITH DELAYS | 6 | 6 |  |
|  | **TOTAL** | **111** | 78 |  |

**AIRLINE: MALAYSIA AIRLINES**

**GRADING OUT OF TEN. BUSINESS CLASS.** ECONOMY CLASS IN RED

| TYPE OF SERVICE | GRADE | | COMMENTS |
|---|---|---|---|
| BOOKING/RESERVATION | 7 | 7 | |
| CHECK IN/ONLINE | 7 | 7 | TERRIBLE AT EUROPEAN AIRPORTS |
| BASE AIRPORT | 8 | 8 | |
| LOUNGE AT BASE AIRPORT | 9 | N/A | CROWDED BUT EXCELLENT |
| TRANSIT FACILITIES E.G. SECURITY CLEARANCE ETC | 8 | 8 | |
| WELCOME ON BOARD | 6 | 6 | |
| SEAT COMFORT | 7 | 6 | |
| AMENITIES | 6 | 5 | |
| CHOICE OF DRINKS | 6 | 5 | |
| FOOD PRESENTATION | 7 | 6 | |
| FOOD VARIETY AND QUALITY | 7 | 5 | |
| ATTITUDE OF STAFF | 8 | 6 | THE ATTITUDE OF FEMALE STAFF IS |
| QUALITY OF STAFF | 5 | 5 | EXCELLENT BUT THE MALE STAFF |
| FACILITIES ON BOARD | 7 | 6 | TEND TO BE RUDE |
| PUNCTUALITY | 7 | 7 | |
| DEALING WITH DELAYS | 5 | 5 | |
| **Total** | **110** | **92** | |

**AIRLINE: GULF AIR**

**GRADING OUT OF TEN. BUSINESS CLASS.** ECONOMY CLASS IN RED

| | TYPE OF SERVICE | GRADE | COMMENTS |
|---|---|---|---|
| | BOOKING/RESERVATION | 7   7 | |
| | CHECK IN/ONLINE | 7   5 | |
| | BASE AIRPORT | 7   7 | |
| | LOUNGE AT BASE AIRPORT | 9   N/A | |
| | TRANSIT FACILITIES E.G. SECURITY CLEARANCE ETC | 8   8 | |
| | WELCOME ON BOARD | 6   5 | |
| | SEAT COMFORT | 6   5 | |
| | AMENITIES | 6   4 | |
| | CHOICE OF DRINKS | 6   5 | |
| | FOOD PRESENTATION | 8   6 | |
| | FOOD VARIETY AND QUALITY | 7   6 | |
| | ATTITUDE OF STAFF | 6   5 | |
| | QUALITY OF STAFF | 6   6 | |
| | FACILITIES ON BOARD | 5   6 | |
| | PUNCTUALITY | 7   7 | |
| | DEALING WITH DELAYS | 7   7 | |
| | **TOTAL** | **108**   89 | |

**AIRLINE: SINGAPORE AIRLINES**

**GRADING OUT OF TEN. BUSINESS CLASS.** ECONOMY CLASS IN RED

| | TYPE OF SERVICE | GRADE | COMMENTS |
|---|---|---|---|
| | BOOKING/RESERVATION | 7   7 | |
| | CHECK IN/ONLINE | 7   7 | |
| | BASE AIRPORT | 7   7 | |
| | LOUNGE AT BASE AIRPORT | 7   N/A | |
| | TRANSIT FACILITIES E.G. SECURITY CLEARANCE ETC | 7   7 | |
| | WELCOME ON BOARD | 7   6 | |
| | SEAT COMFORT | 7   5 | |
| | AMENITIES | 7   5 | |
| | CHOICE OF DRINKS | 8   5 | |
| | FOOD PRESENTATION | 8   6 | |
| | FOOD VARIETY AND QUALITY | 8   5 | |
| | ATTITUDE OF STAFF | 7   6 | |
| | QUALITY OF STAFF | 7   7 | |
| | FACILITIES ON BOARD | 8   8 | |
| | PUNCTUALITY | 8   8 | |
| | DEALING WITH DELAYS | 8   8 | |
| | **TOTAL** | **118**   97 | |

AIRLINE: THAI AIR

**GRADING OUT OF TEN. BUSINESS CLASS.** ECONOMY CLASS IN RED

| | TYPE OF SERVICE | GRADE | | COMMENTS |
|---|---|---|---|---|
| | BOOKING/RESERVATION | 7 | 7 | |
| | CHECK IN/ONLINE | 7 | 7 | |
| | BASE AIRPORT | 6 | 6 | |
| | LOUNGE AT BASE AIRPORT | 5 | N/A | |
| | TRANSIT FACILITIES E.G. SECURITY CLEARANCE ETC | 6 | 6 | |
| | WELCOME ON BOARD | 7 | 6 | |
| | SEAT COMFORT | 7 | 5 | |
| | AMENITIES | 6 | 5 | |
| | CHOICE OF DRINKS | 7 | 5 | |
| | FOOD PRESENTATION | 7 | 6 | |
| | FOOD VARIETY AND QUALITY | 7 | 5 | |
| | ATTITUDE OF STAFF | 6 | 6 | |
| | QUALITY OF STAFF | 6 | 6 | |
| | FACILITIES ON BOARD | 7 | 7 | |
| | PUNCTUALITY | 7 | 7 | |
| | DEALING WITH DELAYS | 6 | 6 | |
| | **TOTAL** | **104** | 90 | |

**AIRLINE: GARUDA**

**GRADING OUT OF TEN. BUSINESS CLASS.** ECONOMY CLASS IN RED

| | TYPE OF SERVICE | GRADE | COMMENTS |
|---|---|---|---|
| | BOOKING/RESERVATION | 7  7 | |
| | CHECK IN/ONLINE | 7  7 | |
| | BASE AIRPORT | 6  6 | |
| | LOUNGE AT BASE AIRPORT | 5  N/A | |
| | TRANSIT FACILITIES E.G. SECURITY CLEARANCE ETC | 6  6 | |
| | WELCOME ON BOARD | 7  6 | |
| | SEAT COMFORT | 7  5 | |
| | AMENITIES | 6  5 | |
| | CHOICE OF DRINKS | 8  6 | |
| | FOOD PRESENTATION | 8  6 | |
| | FOOD VARIETY AND QUALITY | 8  5 | |
| | ATTITUDE OF STAFF | 8  6 | |
| | QUALITY OF STAFF | 7  7 | |
| | FACILITIES ON BOARD | 7  7 | |
| | PUNCTUALITY | 7  7 | |
| | DEALING WITH DELAYS | 6  6 | |
| | **TOTAL** | **110**  92 | |

# AIRLINE: CATHAY PACIFIC

## GRADING OUT OF TEN. BUSINESS CLASS. ECONOMY CLASS IN RED

| | TYPE OF SERVICE | GRADE | COMMENTS |
|---|---|---|---|
| | BOOKING/RESERVATION | 7 7 | |
| | CHECK IN/ONLINE | 7 7 | |
| | BASE AIRPORT | 7 7 | |
| | LOUNGE AT BASE AIRPORT | 7 N/A | |
| | TRANSIT FACILITIES E.G. SECURITY CLEARANCE ETC | 6 6 | |
| | WELCOME ON BOARD | 7 6 | |
| | SEAT COMFORT | 7 5 | |
| | AMENITIES | 6 5 | |
| | CHOICE OF DRINKS | 7 6 | |
| | FOOD PRESENTATION | 7 6 | |
| | FOOD VARIETY AND QUALITY | 8 5 | |
| | ATTITUDE OF STAFF | 6 6 | |
| | QUALITY OF STAFF | 6 6 | |
| | FACILITIES ON BOARD | 7 7 | |
| | PUNCTUALITY | 7 7 | |
| | DEALING WITH DELAYS | 6 6 | |
| | **TOTAL** | **108** 92 | |

# AIRLINE: EVA AIR

## GRADING OUT OF TEN. BUSINESS CLASS. ECONOMY CLASS IN RED

| | TYPE OF SERVICE | GRADE | COMMENTS |
|---|---|---|---|
| | BOOKING/RESERVATION | 7  7 | |
| | CHECK IN/ONLINE | 7  7 | |
| | BASE AIRPORT | 6  6 | |
| | LOUNGE AT BASE AIRPORT | 6  N/A | |
| | TRANSIT FACILITIES E.G. SECURITY CLEARANCE ETC | 6  6 | |
| | WELCOME ON BOARD | 7  7 | |
| | SEAT COMFORT | 7  6 | |
| | AMENITIES | 6  5 | |
| | CHOICE OF DRINKS | 7  6 | |
| | FOOD PRESENTATION | 7  6 | |
| | FOOD VARIETY AND QUALITY | 8  6 | |
| | ATTITUDE OF STAFF | 8  8 | |
| | QUALITY OF STAFF | 8  8 | |
| | FACILITIES ON BOARD | 7  7 | |
| | PUNCTUALITY | 7  7 | |
| | DEALING WITH DELAYS | 6  6 | |
| | **TOTAL** | **110  98** | |

**AIRLINE: CHINA AIRLINES**

**GRADING OUT OF TEN. BUSINESS CLASS.** ECONOMY CLASS IN RED

|  | TYPE OF SERVICE | GRADE | COMMENTS |
|---|---|---|---|
|  | BOOKING/RESERVATION | 6  6 |  |
|  | CHECK IN/ONLINE | 6  6 |  |
|  | BASE AIRPORT | 6  6 |  |
|  | LOUNGE AT BASE AIRPORT | 6  N/A |  |
|  | TRANSIT FACILITIES E.G. SECURITY CLEARANCE ETC | 6  6 |  |
|  | WELCOME ON BOARD | 6  6 |  |
|  | SEAT COMFORT | 7  5 |  |
|  | AMENITIES | 5  5 |  |
|  | CHOICE OF DRINKS | 6  5 |  |
|  | FOOD PRESENTATION | 5  5 |  |
|  | FOOD VARIETY AND QUALITY | 5  5 |  |
|  | ATTITUDE OF STAFF | 6  5 |  |
|  | QUALITY OF STAFF | 5  5 |  |
|  | FACILITIES ON BOARD | 5  5 |  |
|  | PUNCTUALITY | 6  6 |  |
|  | DEALING WITH DELAYS | 6  6 |  |
|  | **TOTAL** | **92  82** |  |

**AIRLINE: CHINA SOUTHERN**

**GRADING OUT OF TEN. BUSINESS CLASS.** ECONOMY CLASS IN RED

| | TYPE OF SERVICE | GRADE | COMMENTS |
|---|---|---|---|
| | BOOKING/RESERVATION | 7  7 | |
| | CHECK IN/ONLINE | 6  6 | |
| | BASE AIRPORT | 5  5 | |
| | LOUNGE AT BASE AIRPORT | 4  N/A | |
| | TRANSIT FACILITIES E.G. SECURITY CLEARANCE ETC | 5  5 | |
| | WELCOME ON BOARD | 6  4 | |
| | SEAT COMFORT | 6  5 | |
| | AMENITIES | 4  3 | |
| | CHOICE OF DRINKS | 5  4 | |
| | FOOD PRESENTATION | 5  5 | |
| | FOOD VARIETY AND QUALITY | 5  5 | |
| | ATTITUDE OF STAFF | 6  5 | |
| | QUALITY OF STAFF | 6  5 | |
| | FACILITIES ON BOARD | 5  5 | |
| | PUNCTUALITY | 5  5 | |
| | DEALING WITH DELAYS | 4  4 | |
| | **TOTAL** | **84  73** | |

**AIRLINE: QATAR AIRWAYS**

**GRADING OUT OF TEN. BUSINESS CLASS. ECONOMY CLASS IN RED**

|  | TYPE OF SERVICE | GRADE | COMMENTS |
|---|---|---|---|
|  | BOOKING/RESERVATION | 7 |  |
|  | CHECK IN/ONLINE | 7 |  |
|  | BASE AIRPORT | 9 |  |
|  | LOUNGE AT BASE AIRPORT | N/A |  |
|  | TRANSIT FACILITIES E.G. SECURITY CLEARANCE ETC | 8 |  |
|  | WELCOME ON BOARD | 7 |  |
|  | SEAT COMFORT | 6 |  |
|  | AMENITIES | 5 |  |
|  | CHOICE OF DRINKS | 6 |  |
|  | FOOD PRESENTATION | 6 |  |
|  | FOOD VARIETY AND QUALITY | 6 |  |
|  | ATTITUDE OF STAFF | 6 |  |
|  | QUALITY OF STAFF | 6 |  |
|  | FACILITIES ON BOARD | 5 |  |
|  | PUNCTUALITY | 7 |  |
|  | DEALING WITH DELAYS | 7 |  |
|  | **TOTAL** | 100 |  |

**AIRLINE: JAPAN AIRLINES**

**GRADING OUT OF TEN. BUSINESS CLASS. ECONOMY CLASS IN RED**

| TYPE OF SERVICE | GRADE | COMMENTS |
|---|---|---|
| BOOKING/RESERVATION | 6　6 | |
| CHECK IN/ONLINE | 6　6 | |
| BASE AIRPORT | 5　6 | |
| LOUNGE AT BASE AIRPORT | 5　N/A | |
| TRANSIT FACILITIES E.G. SECURITY CLEARANCE ETC | 6　6 | |
| WELCOME ON BOARD | 6　6 | |
| SEAT COMFORT | 7　5 | |
| AMENITIES | 4　3 | |
| CHOICE OF DRINKS | 4　4 | |
| FOOD PRESENTATION | 5　5 | |
| FOOD VARIETY AND QUALITY | 5　5 | |
| ATTITUDE OF STAFF | 5　5 | |
| QUALITY OF STAFF | 5　5 | |
| FACILITIES ON BOARD | 3　3 | |
| PUNCTUALITY | 8　8 | |
| DEALING WITH DELAYS | 6　6 | |
| **TOTAL** | **86　79** | |

# SPORT

**Sports do not build character. They reveal it ….. Heywood Broun**

In my opinion Sport and life are intertwined. If one participates in any form of sport, their character is either strengthened or depleted through the success or failure that they may achieve.  If one just watches Sport then it can be a part of the leisure that all human beings need .Watching Sport live or on TV or listening to the commentary on the Radio removes every day tension and mostly gives enjoyment. This should have a positive impact on our characters. Of course disappointments can create short term depression as well. There are human beings who never participate in Sport or take the trouble to watch it. This may be due to a number of reasons and some of these may be very unfortunate e.g. extreme poverty, poor health etc. In other cases it may well be apathy. I believe, most of us are blessed if we have the opportunity to either participate or watch sport.

When I was young, I loved to play Cricket but I was a complete failure at it. I failed most of the time and felt humiliated at other times but I never gave up and from there on I developed the never say die attitude. Later in life, I played Squash and I had more natural ability for that sport. It came easier to me and if it was not for the excess life style that I led in my twenties, I might have achieved more in that sport. Trying to out manoeuvre an opponent at high speed required intense concentration, fitness (of which I had none), competitiveness and the sheer will to win. All those disciplines gave me the will to live and fight and be assertive and competitive, in every professional role that I took on. In later years I tried my luck with Golf. If there is a sport that can destroy a human being mentally then it has to be this one. The sheer thought of putting a small ball in a small hole in four strokes some 400 metres away sounds improbable and most of the time it is just that. However, apart from regular heart breaks this sport did teach me large amounts of patience and discipline which was best needed at this stage in life. This sport is most definitely addictive. Sadly, due to knee problems I had to give that up as well. Nowadays it is just computer games with the grand children!

We are always influenced by sports that are popular in our own environment and that is understandable. Having lived mostly in the warmer countries , I have little interest in sports like cross-country skiing, Alpine skiing, snowboarding, ski jumping, speed skating, figure skating, luge, skeleton, bobsleigh and snowmobiling. Common team sports include ice hockey, curling etc. For a time when I lived in Scotland I quite enjoyed watching live games of Curling. Some of these Winter sports are great to watch even if that can only be on TV. One can witness great natural skills, athletic abilities and the great dedication that goes into reaching the pinnacle of any sport. Winter Olympics and Ice hockey are very popular sports watched by millions on the TV.

The sports that transcend all boundaries and cultures are most definitely, Football/Soccer, Field and Track events, Swimming, Tennis, Basketball and Golf. To a lesser extent there are Squash, Badminton, Rugby, Field Hockey, Table Tennis etc.

There are strength sports like Boxing, different forms of Wrestling and the great variety of increasingly popular Martial arts.

Horse Racing and Show jumping and Equestrian are all high skill and high value sports

There are Elitist sports like Polo played mostly by the rich and the famous.

There are sports which have very little participation but very popular to watch live or on TV e.g. Horse Racing , Formula one and other types of car racing , Motor cycle and cycle racing.

Talking about Sports leads to discussing the great Sportsmen of the past and the current times, it will involve re-counting the very stupendous feats and the broken records and the pulsating moments which remain in the memories after witnessing one or the other.

Mentioning sports evokes imaginations of packed stadiums or other arenas, passionate noise emanating from the spectators, excitement, ambience and perhaps an escape from reality.

I would like to talk about some of the greatest names in sport as a homage to them but of course my knowledge is limited to the sports I am familiar with. There are probably names in the annals of the American history of sport that I am not familiar with.

Some of the greatest Sportsmen and Sportswomen in my time have been:

- Muhammad Ali has been recognized as the greatest sportsman. He was much more than just a boxer, he was an icon who created an impact on a worldwide audience. He was tremendous athlete with poise and grace and blessed with much natural ability.

- Pele is the greatest footballer that graced the game and there are many other contenders but he had the extra ordinary ability to change the course of events in a flash of a second. The other thing was the way he played the sport with the true spirit.

- Maradona is a great talent who played Football but some of the controversies associated with him diminished his greatness. I saw him play live during some of the games in the World Cup 1986. In the quarter Finals vs England he fisted the Ball in the net claiming the infamous 'Hand of God' goal. In the next game vs Belgium which was the semi-final he scored two outstanding goals and demonstrated his extraordinary ability. In the final vs Germany he did not score a goal but in the second half when Germany had made an unexpected comeback to 2-2 and it was increasingly looking as if they would sneak a winner. Maradona found himself in a little bit of space with ball near the half way line and placed the ball perfectly for Valdano to move forward and score the winning goal. The difference in winning or loosing was that split of a second when he seized that opportunity.

- Jahangir Khan dominated Squash like no one ever has or ever will. He did not loose a single match for over six years.

- In Tennis players like Bjorn Borg, Pete Sampras and Roger Federer set new standards. On the female side Billie Jean King , Martina Naratilova and Serena Williams are the greats

- In track and field events of course lately the name of Usain Bolt is at the top for achieving the unbelievable and consistently breaking human speed records. Carl Lewis was another outstanding figure and he had the additional event of the Long Jump in which he excelled as well.

- Roger Bannister of Great Britain was the first person to break the 4 minute mile and needs to be mentioned.

- Although I did not follow NBA at all but in the 90S when switching channels on a visit to the USA I caught a glimpse of Michael Jordan and I became a fan. He was a Sportsman of extraordinary talent and had the ability to make the impossible happen. He always had that extra time in his play to leave opponents watching.

- I always watched Golf and more so in the era of Tiger Woods . The two Golfers who impressed me not only for their ability and success only were of course Jack Nicklaus the greatest Golfer ever and Arnold Palmer who was just Mr.Golf personified. I hope that Tiger Woods will recover and make some form of a comeback and at least exit the sport in a dignified manner.

TEAM SPORTS

- The German Football side of the 2014 World cup has to be considered one of the greatest as they were the first non – Americas team to win the title in the American continent at Rio de Janiero, Brazil. Also, they way they demolished the Brazilian team in their own territory in front of their fans was fairly awesome.

- I have to mention in the list of great teams the England Football side of 1966 which won the trophy after a dramatic final against Germany.

- In spite of their poor performance at the 2014 World Cup the Brazilian Football teams of 1970, 1982 (did not win), 1994 and 2002 played exceptional and the Samba Football. They have won the world Cup five times which is more than any other team.

- While still on the subject of Football / Soccer as a personal choice I would say that the Liverpool Football Club teams of the 70s and 80s were an outstanding bunch of skilled players managed by the best and that is why they just about won every trophy that was available. I can see this statement arousing much passion but the Football is a sport which arouses passion and sometimes it can even turn ugly.

- Being a fan of cricket, I have to mention the best Cricketing side that ever existed and that was the West Indies team from 1979 to 1988. It had the most fearsome fast Bowl attack and had the best ever batsman Viv Richards backed by the prodigious players like Gordon Greenridge, Desmond Hayes and led by the inspirational Clive Llyod. The only other Team that close was the Australian team under Steve Waugh during the late 90s and the early part of this century.

- The British Lions Rugby team of 1974 which toured South Africa must have a place in the hall of fame where they transcended sport and delivered a polite message to the then abhorrent Apartheid regime.

THE KEY ROLE IN SPORT

Apart from the participants the key role in Sport has to be the part played by referees, judges, umpires or whatever title they are given. This is a difficult role meant to provide unbiased decisions on which rest the outcome of all Sporting events. Increasingly, the use of technology has provided some support to these judges and given them the opportunity to rectify mistakes .This role will require intense powers of concentration and in some forms the event has an end with a couple of hours but there are other events like a Cricket Test Match which lasts five days with play in progress a minimum of six hours per day. You have to admire Cricket umpires for their endurance. In the field sports like Soccer, Rugby and different forms of football require the referee to be physically fit as they have to follow the play at speed and move quickly up and down the field and at the same time keep their focus on the game. They do have assistants off the field moving on the line but the referee is the one most exposed and at times have to control the tempers of the players who may become physically threatening towards other players or the referee and his assistants themselves.

This is one of the most thankless jobs and most fans of sport forget the role played by these judges as their focus is on the Sport and their heroes or heroines and the thrill that Sport does provide.

Let us not forget the Coaches , Trainers , Managers and many other who are somewhat behind the scenes but have critical roles to play.

# ANECDOTES AND CURIOUSITIES OF LIFE......

- I just wonder …. As I am a believer and when faced with a life and death crisis I am very pleased that I am one e.g. when travelling by air at 40,000 feet high if the plane hits bad turbulence whereby you can see wings flapping violently and the aircraft almost doing cart wheels, hearing strange noises emanating from within and outside the aircraft, fellow passengers starting to panic. I gain much needed comfort and confidence by praying to the Almighty. I wonder what the non - believers do? Do they just take it all in a cool manner or do they become believers for a short instance?

- Is it my imagination that as you get older the time seems to go by faster? Perhaps this is because sub consciously we know that time is running out.  The realization that there is no second chance makes it harder to accept this swift passage of time.

- When you are very young you cannot wait to grow up and the time really grinds. When you are in the flush of youth, you feel that you are invincible and that era will never end. When you reach the mature years you start to appreciate time gone by and the time left in your life. That is when you feel that time is moving faster

- Someone once told me, **"Perception is reality."** That is the most accurate statement   that I have ever heard in almost the seven decades that I have lived.

- When talking about achievements the word 'Almost' and **'Nearly'** mean nothing it only implies being second best which in most situations is a failure.

# ACKNOWLEDGEMENTS


1.0   AIR TRAVEL WIKEPEDIA
2.0   MEXICO WIKEPEDIA
3.0   AZTECS WIKEPEDIA
4.0   MEXICO TOURISM
5.0   PERU WIKEPEDIA
6.0   MACHU PICCHU WIKEPEDIA
7.0   MALAYSIA WIKEPEDIA
8.0   MALAYSIA TOURISM
9.0   CHINA WIKEPEDIA
10.0   UNITED KINGDOM HISTORY – WIKEPEDIA
11.0   UNITED KINGDOM WIKEPEDIA
12.0   TOURISM UNITED KINGDOM